D0416805

CHRIS JOYNT
THE QUIET MAN

Chris Joynt and Mike Critchley

VERTICAL EDITIONS

Copyright © Chris Joynt and Mike Critchley 2005

The right of Chris Joynt and Mike Critchley to be identified as the authors of this work has been asserted in accordance with the Copyright, Designs and Patents Act, 1988

All rights reserved. The reproduction and utilisation of this book in any form or by any electrical, mechanical or other means, now known or hereafter invented, including xerography, photocopying and recording, and in any information storage and retrieval system, is forbidden without the written permission of the publisher

First published in the United Kingdom in 2005 by Vertical Editions, 7 Bell Busk, Skipton, North Yorkshire BD23 4DT

ISBN 1-904091-11-3

Jacket design and typeset by HBA, York

Printed and bound by The Cromwell Press, Trowbridge

CONTENTS

Dedicated to Nana Maye, Alec Givvons and Geoff Lyon.

Chris Joynt

ACKNOWLEDGEMENTS

I would like to thank my family for their constant backing and Andrea for her love and support over the past 14 years.

I would like to pay tribute to all the coaches and players I have been in contact with during my professional career, and also during my school and amateur days.

And thank all the fans for making my time so special when I was playing.

I have enjoyed writing the book and Larkin's restaurant in North Road, which is one of my favourite haunts, provided us with a great base to work from during the interviews.

I would also like to thank Mike Critchley, photographer's Bernard Platt and Sig Kasatkin, Roger Halstead of the *Oldham Chronicle*, Mike Appleton and Bill Bates for their help in putting the book together.

Chris Joynt

FOREWORD BY
SHAUN EDWARDS

At one stage back in 2001 when it looked likely that I was going to become Warrington Wolves' coach, my first thought was about recruiting a captain.

I needed a player I could rely on, who would be a shining example to the younger players in his attitude, toughness, skill level and the way he conducts his life off the field.

The first person I thought of was Chris Joynt.

As it turned out I never did become Warrington's coach and Chris stayed loyal to Saints, carrying on for another three years to become arguably the most successful skipper in the history that famous club.

His record speaks for itself, but despite winning all those medals, trophies and awards, Chris remains such a humble lad.

His humility and tremendous work ethic are two of his strongest personal characteristics, which have both contributed to his achievements for club and country in 16 seasons as a professional rugby league player.

Over the years Chris has played with devastating effect down his favoured left hand side, using his fantastic turn of speed, left foot step and hand off as weapons to penetrate the most determined of defences.

His partnership with Tommy Martyn, Paul Newlove and Anthony Sullivan terrorised defences and laid the platform for the club's success in the Super League era.

In that quartet, Chris was always to the fore with his tremendous fitness and support play yielding many a try – and he would always still be going strong right until the final hooter.

Consistent Chris's other big strength was his rock solid defence. It was so strong that I used to try and shift play down the other side because we knew Joynty would snuff out any threatening moves on his patch.

I don't think it is any coincidence that Saints were so successful under Chris Joynt's leadership – and his successor Paul Sculthorpe seems to have picked up a few tips from him on the way.

Paul Sculthorpe must have learned a lot from playing under Chris's captaincy, they are both similar in terms of their level headedness and their exceptional fitness levels.

If you want a test of how highly Chris is regarded both in the way he plays the game and how he conducts himself off the pitch, just listen to his fellow professionals.

None of them have a bad word to say about him, which is unusual given how long he has spent at the top of such a highly competitive and confrontational sporting environment.

Chris has used his talents to the full to enjoy a glorious playing career, and I don't doubt that if he decided that he wanted to pursue a coaching career he has the attributes, the knowledge and attention to detail to become highly proficient in that field also.

Like myself, Chris is a St John Fisher old boy. There, school master Steve McLeod taught us to do our best on the field but also the importance of conducting yourself properly off it – Chris has carried that off to the letter.

Chris Joynt: a true professional and a great competitor.

Shaun Edwards
January 2005

1

A RUGBY TOWN

Rugby league is a way of life in Wigan – and I grew up throwing an oval shaped ball about. It became second nature to me really, particularly with the influences around me. My uncles John and Jimmy Maye had played rugby at a decent level with Orrell.

I count myself as lucky really because I was born, on 7 December, 1971, into a loving family which gave me a fantastic start in life. It was also fitting that my birthplace was Billinge Hospital, which is half-way between St Helens and Wigan.

From a sporting point of view there was a real advantage to having one brother, Brendan, 18 months older than me, and the other, Nicholas, 18 months younger than me. It meant I always had a playing companion because we were always at an age where we could compete with each other at football, rugby or cricket in the street outside our house or in the park. All three of us were all treated as individuals and none of us got what you would call preferential treatment. We all had a really good upbringing, growing up in Beech Hill.

My family counts for so much, not just in terms of my sporting career, but also giving us a good grounding throughout my life. My brothers and I have exactly the same outlook on life.

I first started playing rugby league properly at Sacred Heart infant school when I was just seven years old. It seemed the natural thing to do, more so than kicking a round ball about, and I just got into it straight away. We were all into rugby and there was very little football played in Wigan back then. It might be a bit different now with the Latics doing better than in those non-league days.

In the 1970s Wigan meant one thing – rugby league – and even though they were no longer a top side, having spent a season in the

Second Division, the handling code was still king in the town.

I got into the swing of things straight away and my mum, Eileen, didn't flinch much when I came home with the odd bang or graze. She had five brothers and they used to play rugby, so she could cope with me coming home with cuts and bruises. The only thing my mum did kick off about was us all coming home after a match in all our muddy gear. She would make us strip off at the back door and tell us to chuck all our dirty kit into a bucket outside.

It was while I was at Sacred Heart that schoolteacher Dave Mallin introduced me to rugby league properly, teaching me a bit more about the positions and mechanics of the sport. I could not get enough of it, and because I was a touch bigger than the other kids in my age group, I ended up playing for the year above as well as for my own school year.

Today some parents come up and tell me that they think their Billy is playing too much rugby, but when I think back to those days we were either training or playing every day. That is what kids do!

I was playing stand-off back then and other such fancy positions, even kicking goals and putting up the bombs, although they were probably still called 'up and unders' then! It was really enjoyable and my dad, Jim, came to watch when we played the Schools Under-11s Final at Wigan's Central Park ground. He was so chuffed that we had done so well in getting to the final that he bought me a pair of Mitre Minx – which were best boots you could get your hands on at the time. They were the real bees knees of boots.

At about this time I first began getting my name listed in the *Wigan Observer* and the *Evening Post*, which kept my mum busy filling the scrap books, cutting my name and picture out. She has kept hold of them – but I have never been one for hoarding anything like that. She has my whole career in clippings from all the local papers and, once I turned pro, the cuttings from the national press as well.

Schoolboy rugby in Wigan was fiercely competitive – even at junior school level. Although I was only 10, I was having trials for the Under-11s town team, where Mick Mullaney was the coach.

I played most of my schoolboy rugby on the old Robin Park, before they developed it into the sports complex it is today.

But it was not all success and joy and in 1982 I suffered my biggest early disappointment when I missed out on playing at Wembley. Wigan Under-11s were playing against Morley in the Bertie Bassett Challenge, which was one of the centrepieces of the Challenge Cup Final curtain raiser. I was a year younger than that age group, but went for the trials anyway because the town only ever got chance to play at Wembley every blue moon. This would be my only chance – and unfortunately I just missed out on selection. The Wigan side that day included lads like Phil Clarke, Jason O'Loughlin and Gus O'Donnell, who all went on to turn professional. In that game Clarkey put a foot into touch and he was caught on camera crying his eyes out. He was absolutely distraught because the touch judge had disallowed his try. It didn't scar him for life though, as he still went on to skipper Great Britain!

Although I was gutted at missing out, it probably stood me in good stead in the long run. One of the goals I aspired to as a kid was to eventually play at Wembley, but then again what schoolboy does not dream about that?

I settled for a spectator's role that day and a bloke called Frank Webb took me down to watch my first live Challenge Cup Final. It was the drawn game between Hull and Widnes. We caught the bus from outside the Gas Showrooms in Wigan and it was full of family members of the lads who were playing in the curtain raiser. Getting my first glimpse of the Twin Towers and walking down Wembley Way was a fabulous experience. I had watched the previous couple of finals on *Grandstand* and used to love all that build up, but this was something else. I went regularly to the finals after that.

The lads leaving Sacred Heart automatically went to St John Fisher – and I could not have wished to go to a better senior school to continue my rugby learning curve. It really hits you straight away that this is a school steeped in rugby league tradition – and you only have to look at the old boys' roll of honour for confirmation of that. The school teams played the game to a very high standard and it was a respected school in the borough because of that. That rugby pedigree fitted in with me just fine.

I started at St John Fisher in 1983, the year that Shaun Edwards had left to turn professional. Everyone at the school had watched Alex Murphy signing him for Wigan in front of the *Breakfast TV* cameras and that sent a real buzz around the school.

Our school had a hall of fame – Mike Gregory, Ged Byrne and Jeff Clare had all turned pro – and one of my goals when I saw that was to become part of it one day. My big influence at the school was Head of Games, Steve McLeod, who had taught those players and had a kind of fear factor attached to him – and sometimes he would test you out.

You can tell when rugby becomes something more than throwing a ball about when you actually go home thinking about the game you have just played in and what else you could have done to win it.

Although I was still playing for enjoyment, as a player I was developing a more competitive edge. It brought its rewards and, following trial after trial, I ended up getting picked to play for the Lancashire U13 schoolboys. One of my early county games was against a Yorkshire side containing future Bradford Bulls skipper, Steve McNamara.

At school level our big rivals were Wigan Deanery and St Thomas More, who had an abundance of players who were also playing for the town team and Lancashire.

My school, St John Fisher, were probably the top team in Wigan, and enjoyed plenty of success. One of the many highlights there was at Under-16 level when we beat Yorkshire champions, Castleford High School, in the final at Central Park. That night I packed down in the back row with future Wigan forward, Mick Cassidy, in the second row. Paul Anderson, later of Bradford and Great Britain fame, was propping for Castleford – and even back then he was huge.

It was the third time our school had won the trophy – with Jeff Clare and Shaun Edwards being the previous skippers.

My first England call-up came for the schoolboy Under-16s and we went to France with coach Dennis McHugh, a teacher from Golborne, who took England schoolboys for many years.

I had never been abroad before and although I enjoyed the trip what I remember most about France, and still hate about it today, is that I ended up being hungry because all I ate over there was bread! When the meat comes over it is always rare looking and bloody and I am not into anything like that. As a kid I thought, 'I am not eating that. It is probably horse meat'.

I was over there for a week and we played three games.

Playing in France then put me in good stead for the future. The French are confidence players and if you let them get off to a good start they can show you a thing or two. But they also lack a bit of ticker too when the going gets tough and you get ahead of the game.

After that I remember thinking, 'I am an international,' which is really full-on stuff at that age.

Everybody got a suit and we had to do a bit of fund raising for it. It was the same for Lancashire – if you wanted the jumper you had to pay £13. So it was always a case of getting the raffle tickets out! It was a lot of money then, especially because my two brothers were also playing.

Apart from schoolboy rugby, I also played at a junior club. I went down to St Jude's Under-10s with John Sharples, who I had played the majority of my rugby with at school. We were probably in the first crop of youngsters at the club and it really boomed from there. I played there up to under-14s level and then I joined St Pat's. All I did then was play rugby – once in midweek for the school, for the town team on the Saturday and for my club St Jude's or St Pat's on the Sunday.

On top of that we had training for all three teams during the week. It was bizarre because I used to play against somebody for the school on Wednesday, train and play alongside them for the next two days, and then end up playing against them on the Sunday for a different team!

There were some really tense encounters, particularly at Under-16 and Under-17 levels, and I recall a stage when everyone was talking about turning professional. About that time St Pat's played Waterhead five times in six weeks – they had a certain Barrie McDermott propping for them. I enjoyed some good tussles with him along the way.

Amateur rugby at that stage was very competitive, even more so with the parents! Often the parents are even worse than the lads – games were sometimes abandoned because of the different things happening on the touchline, which always marred what rugby was all about.

I was pretty fortunate with regards my training and development because I was getting good coaching on all sides – the school, Lancashire and St Jude's under the supervision of Tommy Martindale, John Toohey and Barry Cornish. These volunteer coaches are invaluable to rugby league – they have a massive influence on the game and they have no qualms about giving their time up freely.

It is hard for teenagers today to keep out of trouble. But the way we kept out of lumber was by always doing something, usually with a rugby ball. We had no time to get up to mischief.

The discipline was a big thing, even things like getting to training, which was a three mile walk for me. There was no 'drop us off here, Dad, I am going to training!' It was competitive, but enjoyment was the big thing. And because there were fewer teams, we had further to travel. Jumping on a mini-bus to go to Saddleworth on a Sunday morning was like a day out for us.

It all put us on a good footing, especially as everything was not geared up to simply winning. If I go to watch a junior game now, it seems to be a case of give the ball to the biggest lad and he'll score. We were not like that and our games were more about enjoyment until that certain age. A win was a bonus.

St Jude's didn't have a clubhouse then, just two pitches, a concrete dressing shed for home and away teams and a lock up for the balls and tackle bags. That's all.

I went to St Pat's when I was 14 which was the top amateur club at the time – all the lads who were playing with the town team and Lancashire were all there. It was like, 'Come on Joynty, come down here with us'. So I ended up going to Pat's, which was no different than St Jude's, although they had just had a clubhouse built.

Quite a few St Pat's lads ended up turning professional. I played a lot of my junior rugby with stand-off Andrew Fairclough, who had a spell with Saints before going on to Salford and Leigh. There were also a few other lads who ended up playing at professional level: Iyan Green, who had a spell at Saints, Aiden Halliwell and Neil Dutson. We had a good team there under the guidance of coaches like Eddie Gallagher.

I was conscious that I had a talent at that age, but I didn't go to St Pat's deliberately to get picked up by professional clubs – I was only 14 when I went. In the years before me, players like Mike Gregory (Warrington), Andy Gregory (Widnes) and Andy Platt (Saints) had all been snapped up while at St Pat's. Some lads like Richard Russell and Tim Street came over to Pat's from Oldham, presumably with a view to getting signed up and both ended up turning pro with Wigan.

Before a game you used to hear a few whispers that Derek Standish, a scout for Wigan, and Billy Wilkinson, who picked up players for Widnes, were on the touchline. They were always stood together and they used to watch us because they knew all the talent was there. Then they were only interested in 16 and 17-year-olds, but nowadays professional clubs are picking lads as young as 12.

So as you can see, rugby was my focus in and out of school. Although school was enjoyable, if I had my time over again I think I had it in me to make more of my educational opportunities. The teachers would always put comments on my reports like, 'Rugby is not everything!' I knew maybe it was not, but that is what I wanted to do. If I had listened to them I could have left school with more than my five GCSEs, but I still had ambition.

When I was at school there were a lot of strikes and other industrial action going on, which meant we used to be sent home at different times because the teachers were missing. We had a sheet with our eight lessons on and if we had no teacher between 11am and 12, we would cross the next two out as well and then say, 'There is no point going back now!' We used to do little tricks like that – I never wagged school, we were always smart enough to get a reason for not going.

I guess I had rugby tunnel vision, but I have only now realised that everyone was probably right telling me to knuckle down. Anything can happen when you play this game – what would have happened had I picked up a bad injury when I was 21 and not played again?

One thing I did pass when I was 16 and still at school was the Rugby League National Coaching Scheme's Preliminary Coaching Certificate, which was part of our GCSE in PE. I got a Grade One pass.

By the time I had finished my exams I had already got a job lined up and served my apprenticeship as a plasterer. My mum's brother, my Uncle John, took me on board and after I left school I worked as a labourer, mixing for him. I always maintain that this is where I got my stomach muscles from, not through sit-ups, but through raking up browning out of tin baths. It was hard graft and I did it for quite a few years. I know people from the building trade come up to me nowadays and say, 'Joynty, you used to be a plasterer …' My response is, 'Well in my day, we had it hard. We had to use a rake and a tin bath, not these fancy drills you have to mix the stuff with nowadays'.

I could still plaster a room today – it is not a skill you lose overnight. In fact I have picked up my tools a few times in recent years to help out with The Prince's Trust charity that I am involved with. I have plastered various walls and ceilings with them. The last one I did was a bathroom in Sutton for a chap who had had a motorbike accident half way through having his house renovated. They sent The Prince's Trust in to assist and I got a phone call asking me to sort his walls out. When I finished he was so chuffed that he asked me to sign the walls because it meant so much to him.

I was not just playing rugby – much as Saints fans will not like reading this – I used to spend an awful lot of time watching Wigan in the 80s. They were boom years at Central Park. When I started I used to get a free ticket from Dave Mallen and Frank Webb at junior school and used to go to every home game. Wigan were just taking off again after a spell in the doldrums. They had won the Cup after a gap of 20 years and were on a real roll, especially after that Wembley win. I remember getting on the coach from the Gas Showrooms with a Wigan hat and scarf on for that win over Hull that day in 1985. The stars that day were Brett Kenny and John Ferguson – two of the best Aussies who have ever come over. Stand-off Kenny was as cool as they come, strutting around in the line-up with his hands in his tracksuit pockets as they called the teams out. Even at that time I was thinking, 'He doesn't look so nervous'.

Shaun Edwards played full-back that day – he had played there the year before, becoming the youngest man to play at Wembley. Me and my schoolmates watched Shaun closely, because he had just left our school.

When watching a game then I didn't really focus on the players playing in my position. I was like everyone, press included, just watching who was making breaks and scoring the tries. That is why Kenny and Ferguson stuck in my head, because they ran riot in 1984–85.

Wigan had the best team money could buy; it was probably like watching Manchester United when they were winning everything. We were following a team we thought were never going to lose.

The crowds there were massive too then and that is one of the things that used to spur me on. I used to stand in the corner between the Kop and the Popular Side among crowds of 20,000, thinking, 'How good it would be to play in front of that every week'. What a difference that was to playing in front of 10 blokes and a dog at St Pat's or St Jude's.

Because we were Catholics, on the way back from a game we used to go St Mary's and St John's Church which was at the top of the ginnel you walked through after leaving Central Park. We would only get out of the ground at about quarter to five, so by the time we crept into the back of the church 20 minutes had gone, so the service flew by. Next minute it was offertory, hymns and away we were. Still we had been if anyone ever asked us!

At 16 we were still getting free tickets to get into Wigan, but we began getting hassle at the turnstiles because we looked older than schoolboys and I started drifting away. When it came down to it, I always preferred playing to watching and anyway the novelty had worn off. At that age you also begin to have other things on your mind.

One of my worst memories of being a Wigan fan, ironically came after a Good Friday game at Knowsley Road in 1986 when I was 15. The trains were not running and going back me and my mates lost our bearings in the town centre when we were looking for the bus stop for Wigan.

This lad, seeing we were lost, came over and asked, 'Do you know where the Wigan bus stop is?' Once we told him that was what we were looking for, he gave a loud whistle and all his mates came running out of an alleyway to give us a bit of a kicking.

All those years I played in Saints v Wigan games afterwards, I have often driven past the crowds wondering if those lads still go to the match and if they know who it was they attacked! Still, it demonstrated starkly what the biggest derby rivalry in rugby league was all about!

2

SNOW, HILLS AND NOEL EDMONDS

Widnes were the first club to approach me while I was at St Pat's, followed by Swinton and then Saints, who invited me to go to their summer school.

At that time I was already training with Wigan's development team, of which half the players were from the amateur set-up and the others were professionals. They included Mike Forshaw, Peter Moran, Gus O'Donnell and Ian Gildart and we trained up on the top pitch at Central Park, which is now the fruit and veg aisle of Tesco's.

I can still remember the game that secured me a pro contract – it was for Lancashire U17s against Yorkshire at the long since demolished Station Road ground, Swinton. Both of the Barrow brothers were there watching – Frank was coaching Swinton at the time and Oldham coach Tony was there because his son, Tony junior, was playing for Lancashire.

The game went well for me and I won the man of the match award. Straight after the game you can imagine the scene; Frank was into me in one ear, while Tony was really having a go in the other. I was oblivious to what was going on around me and what was being said and offered. There was still talk of other teams coming in for me and I had already spoken to Wigan scout Derek Standish about going to Central Park.

If Wigan wanted a top class back rower in the late 80s or early 90s, they would search the world for one. It was the same for the other positions as well, and there were a lot of Wigan lads like Gus O'Donnell, Wayne Reid, Mike Forshaw and an abundance of others who were just stuck in the A team. They had a fantastic A team but none of them ever got a decent crack at the first team.

It was my decision therefore, to sign for what some would deem an unfashionable club, Oldham. I thought to myself that if I am to become any good at this game I might as well learn my trade elsewhere because I had seen what had happened to these lads who had signed for Wigan.

Even though I knew Oldham didn't have the money and resources Wigan had available, I knew I would get the breaks there. Oldham at that time were buying a lot of young players and were building a decent set up at The Watersheddings.

Having played most of my junior career with Tony Barrow Jnr, I always knew his dad and his involvement with professional rugby league. I had got to know him well and I respected what he said. He was honest and when I was weighing up my options he asked, 'Why do you want to go to Wigan, Widnes or St Helens? You will chance a lot quicker here'. That was on the lines that I was thinking too.

My parents knew there were clubs sniffing around me, but they left the decision entirely up to me. The money was an issue. My parents had taught me the value of money really and I was being offered somewhere between £5,000 and £8,000 to sign on for four years, which was a lot to me then, at 17 going on 18.

I visited The Watersheddings a few times and took a real liking to it. It was a quirky little place and the first thing you saw was the dog track around the back of the rugby pitch. It always seemed to be a hive of activity, a really busy place.

They had the training ground at the side of the stand, which I had already experienced playing on with Lancashire schoolboys. And then there was also something that resembled an old cricket pavilion tucked away round one corner. You just would not get a ground designed like that today, it was unique.

Inside was like a rabbit warren, with that many doors and corridors. The first thing I learned there was that you never went into the first team dressing room unless you had been invited in, that was something I was told on my first day by kit man Alec Givvons.

Alec had been an absolute legend of a player, and he became one of my best mates at the Watersheddings. No matter who you were – John Cogger, Brett Clarke or Joe Bloggs Jnr – everybody got treated the same way by Alec. He used to get your kit washed and pressed and put on your peg for you.

He became a good friend to me and he was my mentor when I had to start making big decisions in life and in my career. This continued long after I had left Oldham, including when I was playing for Great Britain and captaining Saints. Alec lived on Watersheddings Street, right next to the ground, and was always there to give me advice.

Alec was a real gentleman – and one that always had time for you. He would always have good, sensible words for you. Time is a really precious thing in life, and he gave his time to me selflessly and passed on some great advice and was always a good pair of ears for me. I could sit with him for hours.

I remember him saying to me when I was at Saints, 'Joynty, don't take the captaincy on son'. Alec was a great bloke – a legend.

At Oldham we trained every Tuesday and Thursday night, and I had more reasons than most to dread that first session. It was a big day for me – I had my driving test in the morning and was training with Oldham in the evening. Passing the test was the easy bit and I was bricking it at the prospect of having to drive to Oldham! You don't go on the motorway during your driving lessons, and here I was, barely a couple of hours after passing my test, heading down Death Valley, making my debut on the M61 and M62!

I went straight into the Oldham A team. The set-up was a lot different then, because A teams were used not simply for young players but many contained first teamers who had suffered a dip in form or were recovering from injury.

I can recall some of my early games in the A team playing alongside former Great Britain internationals like John Fieldhouse and Des Foy.

There would be big crowds too – gates of 1,000 plus were not uncommon at the Watersheddings, and as daft as it sounds, some speccies would actually prefer to watch the A team play than the first team. Oldhamers are really passionate about their rugby and there used to be one bloke in particular called Harry Brierton, who used to go to every game, home and away, first team as well as A team. He used to shout, 'Go on Jonty lad!' I don't think he ever called me Joynty!

In my view, there was nothing wrong with that A team system – it was better than this Academy Under-21 set they have in place now. If you were not picked for the first team you automatically played A team rugby. The other massive incentive for me was that I could play my way into the first team panel with a good game in the second string.

I was working as an apprentice plasterer at the time and that income was supplemented by my rugby money, which in the A team was £35 for winning and nothing for losing.

Under Tony Barrow's regime, the best two A team players from Thursday night got squad spots for the Sunday first team game. So you trained with them on the Saturday and would have to rub the first teamers down before the game. In return you received £150 which was half of the first teamers' money, even though you didn't play. So that was a massive incentive and kept me going.

In the A team I played in some really tough games with and against players who I had really looked up to. I remember playing against Shaun Wane – this is a bloke I had watched some years previously take the man of the match for Wigan in that awesome World Club Challenge win over Manly. All of a sudden I was running at him! Wigan flier Mark Preston also cropped up in another game at Central Park. Former Saints, Bradford, Warrington and Great Britain half-back Ken Kelly played in the second row alongside me one week. There is a quiz question knocking about – Which former Saints player has played in the same team as both Tom Van Vollenhoven and Chris Joynt? Well that was Ken Kelly.

Ken was a good mate of Tony Barrow and was a good experienced player looking for a game of rugby. If you had an old head in the side it was always a bonus really, because they used to show you the ropes. Good, old players would put you through gaps that they no longer had the legs for, but they also looked after you as well. It was a tough step up after playing junior football, all of a sudden you are playing against blokes from two to ten years older than you.

In one match I remember our forward John Fairbank giving

Halifax's massive prop Brendan Hill a bit of a facial in the tackle. Well Hill thought it was me that had done it and the next time he got hold of me he got my head between his knees and just squeezed it as hard as he could, shouting in a high-pitched voice, 'Don't mess with me you little bastard!'

Although there was a big difference between playing with the Under-17s and Open Age pro level, your body changes and begins to toughen up in time. We were very fit as well, because we all had manual jobs, were training two nights a week and did our own weight sessions.

Combining work with training was tough, but I was lucky because I was with my uncle John. We used to do up the hotels in Blackpool, plastering the rooms and what have you. Our normal working day would involve setting out from Wigan at 6am, starting work at 7am, knocking off at 4pm to get me back to Wigan just before 5pm.

I would dash in, change quickly and then set off for training at Oldham five minutes later. I would get back home just after 9 o'clock, have my tea and then go to bed. After all that I never had trouble sleeping.

The motorway to Oldham was terrible then, but I used to take it in turns driving over with another Wiganer, Trevor Croston.

One of Tony Barrow's oppos, Bill Kindon, was Oldham's fitness coach and he was like a sergeant major. We were very fit because they had just invested in a track made up of wood-chippings. They got the idea from a system they used to train racehorses on. They put it at the side of the training pitch and it was four lanes wide by 90 metres long. Even back then there would be hundreds watching training which gave you an incentive to train well because you would see all these little heads bobbing over the fence watching us.

Training regimes seem to have gone full circle now. Everybody seems to be going back to the old school fitness drills they put us through in the late 80s. It is different in one way because players are full-time now and have more time to spend on their core skills. But in terms of fitness, those old drills are definitely back in vogue.

Oldham is the worst place in the world for weather – it is always cold – and during the winter if the frozen training pitch would not take a stud at training, they would send us on road runs instead. Well Oldham is not the flattest town in the world, is it?

We used to do a lot of hill running and at pre-season the warm-up to training was running up a place called Count Hill at the side of the Watersheddings. Some people had difficulty walking up it, never mind running. We would be knackered and looking up saying, 'we are not even there yet.'

Watersheddings was the coldest ground in the league. It was always freezing and wet, but we got used to that, so when the opposition used to come and think, 'What are we doing here?' We used that to our advantage.

The Roughyeds would nurture a lot of young players and then sell them on for financial reasons and tended to get a reputation as a bit of a feeder club.

They were always a bit of a yo-yo side in a way, being relegated from the First Division one year, but then bouncing back up the next. I signed when they had just been relegated after 1988–89. So we had a season in the Second Division, then we were promoted again. I was in the A team for roughly the first two years, only getting the odd first team start.

It felt as though I was doing OK, because I was doing plenty of squadding with the first team and was still young.

Some of my best mates still live in Oldham, like Paddy Mitchell, Craig Mort and Richard Pachniuk. We were all as thick as thieves when we were in the A team together.

We still knock about together today. If those lads had the same amount of luck that I had in the game, they could have been Super League players. They had the talent. Craig Mort captained England schoolboys at 16, but it did not then work out for him, which is a shame. They have always been really supportive of me in my career.

Morty and Paddy's parents looked after me when I was in Oldham. Ken and Margaret Mort and Eileen and Gerry Mitchell really watched out for me.

One of the funniest spells I had while I was at Oldham was spending an off-season Down Under in a place called Yenda with a couple of those lads. It was during the spell that I was on the verge of breaking into the first team and Peter Tunks was coach. He thought it would be a good idea to send three of us over to toughen us up. It should have been myself, Paddy Mitchell and Craig Mort because we were all muckers together. But Craig injured himself so Richard Pachniuk ended up taking his place.

Oldham and former Saints half-back Brett Clarke had put an advert in *Rugby League Week* magazine saying, 'Three young professionals looking for a club for the summer,' and we got about three offers.

We opted to play for Yenda, which is in Group 20 in Australia, probably about 20 kilometres from a place called Griffith in New South Wales. It is a massive wine growing region of Australia.

It was a fabulous experience – we were used to living at home getting spoon-fed by our mams and then all of sudden we were 12,000 miles from home, looking after ourselves in the back room of a hotel. Yenda paid us a few hundred dollars and put us up.

The team had never won before we arrived, but we had a win on our debuts and that set the tone for the rest of our stay.

You get all these student kids now going on gap year backpacking holidays – but I don't think there would be many takers for some of the jobs we were doing in Australia.

We were in the middle of nowhere, pruning vines, cleaning the wine vats out, marking lambs, cutting their tails off and any other loose bits! It was fabulous and the rugby was a bonus.

The pitches were rock hard, just like dustbowls. A match day is a big day of rugby over there with the Under-17s playing each other, followed by the 19s and then the main game and everyone turns up. We were like mini celebrities being three Poms, but we were also three sitting ducks when it came to dishing it out. Looking back that was the reason we went over – to toughen us up.

Off the pitch it was fabulous – especially for teaching me some life skills. I have been out there since and met up with some of the folk I knew then and they treat you like a king.

I was never tempted to stay over there mind – four months was enough for me because I did miss my mum and dad. There was a strong pull back home, but I came back a better person and better rugby player.

Probably one of my first games in the first team was on the subs bench at Headingley in 1990–91. I was really nervous, but I didn't get on. After all that I was gutted in the end that I didn't play, because I had lived through the game.

After Tony Barrow left as coach, John Fieldhouse had a short spell in charge. Then former Aussie prop Peter Tunks took over the coaching reins in April 1991 just as I was just beginning to play regular first team rugby.

Tunksy had a big influence on me – he was highly respected because he had played the game at the highest level in Australia. He inherited a good first team, but also a very strong A team. However, he used to give me, Timmy Street and Richard Russell some right good floggings in training up Count Hill.

The unfortunate thing with Tunksy was he was always too busy working out how to get rid of different players and bring in new ones. He ended up getting the nickname Noel Edmonds, because he was a 'Swap Shop' merchant. He would have swapped his granny if he could get two players for her – and I was a pawn in a lot of that exchange talk. My name was linked to every club in the rugby league at one stage.

I would get to training on a night and Tunksy used to pull me to one side and say, 'You are going to Halifax this week'. And I am thinking to myself 'I am not, you know'.

It was probably naughty at the time, but Saints were already after me.

I suppose all the swapping was a case of him trying to build his team the way he wanted it. Forward Paul Round was a good player, club captain and he was like lightning running with the ball, but he was in the twilight of his career.

We all knew what Roundy could do and we took that for granted – I was only just coming through and I used to read reports in the *Oldham Chronicle* comparing me to former Oldham internationals, Bob Irving or Andy Goodway. I was the new kid on the block who people were suddenly talking about.

We had some big names in that side at the time – Charlie McAllister, John Henderson, Mike Ford, Richard Irving and John Cogger.

Assisting Tunksy with the coaching we had Eric Fitzsimmons,

who was more like a schoolteacher or drills coach. Oldham were very lucky, and still are to this day, that they have some outstanding coaches at school level. It is a similar town to Wigan, where everyone has been taught how to play the game. You can tell a Wigan kid by the way he has been coached and Oldham is exactly the same. Former Fulham and Workington winger Iain MacCorquodale was responsible for putting a lot of Oldham lads through, including Paul Sculthorpe and Iestyn Harris. You can tell – they are good footballers and all had good core skills from an early age.

At Oldham I came across a player I would come to develop a fantastic rapport with during my career – Tommy Martyn.

Tommy joined Oldham a touch earlier than I did and they probably signed about ten good up-and-coming youngsters at that time. You knew that something was going to happen with the quality they were bringing in. We played in the A team together and then Tommy played first team a good 12 months before me, while I was just bobbing in and out.

I remember watching Tommy in the Second Division Premiership Final against Hull KR at Old Trafford he did something really spectacular. He scored a try after coming off the bench, and then did handstands across the pitch to celebrate. He was an off-the-cuff, skilful player, and the more his career progressed, the more he became a team player. Tommy always had that instinctive touch in him to do what he could to turn a game. I was very fortunate to play in his company.

From my own point of view, the game that was memorable was a Regal Trophy game against Saints at The Watersheddings that we only narrowly lost. Being a Second Division side Oldham were supposed to have no chance, with Saints bringing their best team. We gave them a real run for their money and I remember breaking through a few times and but for Richard Irving dropping about three sitters on the wing we would have won.

It was a massive game for us. Everyone was up for it and Saints got off to a poor start and we grew a leg, playing some good football. There was a tremendous atmosphere, with nearly 6,000 packed in there, but there was always a good buzz generated at The Watersheddings.

It was funny in the clubhouse afterwards because Frankie Barrow had joined Saints as Mike McClennan's coaching assistant. Straight after the game he was into me straight away and I remember Mike saying to Frankie, 'You can't be doing this. Not in his own clubhouse!'

That is when Saints got to me, they had my number and had made that first contact. After that game I was as good as gone. So when Tunksy came up and said, 'You are going to Halifax!' I knew in my own mind I was going to Saints. One week he threatened me with, 'You are going to Halifax next week or you will be playing A team rugby for the rest of your career'.

I was cocky enough to say, 'Well if that is the case, I will have to play in the A team' because I knew I was sorted.

After that, I got another call from Tunksy with a further inducement and he said, 'You are going to Halifax because I want players X, Y and Z, and the club will pay for a new car for you'.

I couldn't get my head round it, and was thinking this should not be happening really if I am supposed to be their next big thing. I was linked with a load of other clubs, including Castleford and Leeds, but at that stage it was not only me going everywhere, all the other players were linked with other clubs on a daily basis.

All this talk just spurred me on, because until contracts are signed you are only as good as your next game. Just because I played well in that Regal Trophy game didn't mean I could sit back and wait for Saints' offer.

That year we made it through to the Stones Bitter Second Division Premiership final, but unfortunately we lost to Sheffield Eagles after having Ian Sherratt sent off early on in the game. It was my first taste of a big final as a professional and former Wigan player Ged Byrne had an absolute blinder for us at loose forward that day. Although we pegged the Eagles back we just did not have that killer punch or enough in the tank with being a man down.

Sheffield were a very good side in those days with the likes of future internationals Dale Laughton, Paul Broadbent and Hugh Waddell in the forwards. Daryl Powell got a hat-trick for them that day, which proved to be the difference. It was a great experience, played as a curtain raiser to the Saints v Wigan Premiership Final.

The crowd filled up towards the end, because they had turned up for the main event – but before that I remember seeing the gaps in the crowd.

We actually had to get changed at Old Trafford cricket ground that day and had to get the bus to the ground. By the time we returned to the pavilion and got changed I don't think we even watched the main game.

I have still got a real soft spot for Oldham – it was there where I met my girlfriend Andrea in 1990 and we are still together now. I still have a lot of friends there, it's a really friendly town that loves rugby league. Also, Oldham folk probably have a more laid back approach to life. They all like to play and go out for a few pints. I think it is their outlook as individuals – not just the people who I played with.

My first Great Britain Under-21 international call-up came while I was still at Oldham. I was on the bench against Papua New Guinea, which was quite an honour, given I was playing for a Second Division side at the time. It was also a good call financially because I was not on much money and we got £3,000 each – but only if you played. I was subbing and with about 20 minutes left on the clock I was still on the bench and I kept hinting to coach Phil Larder that I wanted to get on. Who wouldn't with three grand riding on it?

That was a good 21s side with lads like Alan Hunte, Gary Connolly and Paul Newlove, who would become the backbone of the full test team in years to come. Phil Clarke skippered us for the games against France and I still look back on those days with really fond memories.

I had been an England schoolboy and that was fantastic. I then set my new goals: become a professional, get in the first team and then the GB Under-21s. They were realistic goals that I was setting and achieving. They were good times for me.

3

THE WRONG
LITTLE CHEF

I signed for Saints in the summer of 1992, just before their Charity Shield game against the previous season's double winners, Wigan, at Gateshead. I didn't play in that game because there were still a few things to iron out first and a few minor details to sort out.

It all nearly went wrong because I had instructions to meet Saints directors Tom Ellard and Mally Kay at the Little Chef on the East Lancashire Road – I didn't realise there was more than one!

Well I was sat there at the Little Chef at Boothstown, waiting and wondering, thinking they were not going to turn up. I was gutted as I sat there gazing into the bottom of my empty tea cup, thinking Saints had changed their mind and the deal had fallen through.

But in those pre-mobile phone days, the two directors were sitting in the Little Chef at Haydock thinking it was me who had changed my mind and was not coming. Still it was resolved – after a bit they rang the restaurant I was waiting in on the off-chance that I was there. It is hilarious now, but wasn't at the time – I could see my career going out of the window.

The discussions and even wranglings between the clubs had been going on for a few months, so it was great when I finally put pen to paper for Saints – a club that was always there or thereabouts for the big finals. It was a dream move for me, and although it was also decent money, I carried on working as a plasterer.

While playing at Oldham I had developed a little bit of a name for myself, but I had not really proved anything. My family was great about me signing for Saints, although I got plenty of reaction from Wigan locals about signing for the old rivals. Still, in a way, many of them were on my side saying, 'Another bloody good young Wigan lad going elsewhere'.

Although a lot of players probably thought Wigan was the place to go to win medals, I was mindful of the large number of talented players who could not get in the side and were rotting in the A team

Going to Saints seemed the right place to go to and they had some tremendous players. Director Mally Kay should take a lot of credit because he has a way with people and brought some fabulous players to the club. He was the sort of bloke who was always on the phone, reassuring you that everything was all right and keeping you in the picture with what was going on.

In many ways Saints was similar to Oldham in terms of my daily routine with regards to working then training and playing. Knowsley Road then used to be a Mecca for people watching training sessions on that front pitch under the orange lights – and they were always keen on checking on the progress of the new lads.

Understandably I was quite nervous about coming to a new club with all the great players who I respected. In those days they used to have a home and an away dressing room at Saints and you had to be invited into the first team dressing rooms. The first time I arrived there I put my bag between Les Quirk and Paul Loughlin and they had a quiet word – I had to be invited in. So the next time I went training, I went to the away team dressing room to change and stayed there.

The only first teamer who was in the away team dressing room then was Bernard Dwyer, who used to sit behind the door. I really respect Bernard or Barney Rubble as they used to call him. He was a fantastic bloke with no edge on him at all. He would play anywhere, number 10, hooker, second row or loose forward. And he could kick goals as well.

With this dressing room business, perhaps Bernard thought the same way as me. I went on to captain the club, but never went into that first team dressing room. It is a different thing now – those days have gone and it is a free for all in the new changing rooms.

It is always a little bit awkward when you move in on somebody else's patch and I made my debut from the bench against Wakefield. Long-serving Paul Forber was still in the second row, but I was after his spot really. It is one of those things – there comes a time in everyone's career when even the most loyal of servants have to move on. 'Buffer' had been there for all those years and maybe because I was the new kid on the block he, understandably, was not as friendly because I was after his jersey.

Rugby league in those days was a 13 man game – the two subs were not used as frequently. I remember benching for a couple of games early on and being gutted, but my dad would say, 'Don't worry about that as long as you get the same money!'

It was an eye-opener and an education sitting on the bench next to Saints' larger than life assistant coach Frankie Barrow. There was a telephone next to the dugouts which coach Mike McClennan used to ring to give Frankie the orders from the box. Well the phone would go every couple of minutes, to the extent that Frankie had enough. Every now and then he would answer the phone and leave it off the hook dangling. You could still hear Mike ranting and raving down the line, but Frankie would carry on watching the game, not listening to him.

Skippering the side we had Shane Cooper who was one of those very gifted players. If you looked at him there is no way that you would have thought he was a rugby player because he only looked 9 stone wet through, but he had a really good brain on him. He was good to play alongside because of his experience, skill and ability to read how a game was going.

Because we were part-time, our routine would be to train, get into the big bath and then have a few drinks afterwards in the club where Kevin and Sheila Whittle ran the bar.

Me and Coops used to have this little competition between ourselves. Whoever was first to drop the ball in training used to have to get all the Guinness and black in that night. You can imagine Coops, he was sending low passes at my feet all evening so he didn't have to get the ale in! On balance it probably turned out about 60/40 in his favour.

During that first year I was able to strike up a good rapport with the other Wigan lads who had come over at the same time – Dave

Lyon and Gus 'Ducky' O'Donnell. Dave's dad, Geoff Lyon, joined the coaching staff in 1995 and he used to drive us over – although we tried to take it in turns.

I have to give Dave Lyon a lot of credit, because at times he has been kind of a mentor for me in terms of keeping me on the straight and narrow. We have always trained together, even when we were not at the same club we have kept in contact. When I have needed advice I have always looked to Dave.

His dad Geoff unfortunately passed away last year and he is sadly missed. He was a great bloke.

I also got on well with lads I had already played alongside for Great Britain Under-21s – Alan Hunte and Gary Connolly. Within four months of playing at Saints I got my first England call-up, being picked on the bench against Wales at Swansea. That was another box ticked!

Kiwi coach McClennan prided himself on his innovation and the year previously he had pioneered big John Harrison 'heading' the ball to score a try. This time, to give us a bit more of an edge in the tackling front, he had fetched over this cast-iron 'power sled' from New Zealand. It consisted of a steel prong with a spring and tackling bag attached to it. We had to hit it up and down the field, which was supposed to do our tackling the world of good.

Well, big Kevin Ward hit the bag so hard in the first session that the sled spun around, flew into the air with the steel shaft snapping clean in half before coming down in pieces.

We couldn't believe it – this machine was supposed to be indestructible.

Wardy just turned round and said, 'That's rubbish that! You'll have to pack it up for scrap iron!'

Although McClennan gave me my chance to play for Saints, on training nights he used to keep me out for extra sessions because I was the new boy. So once the others had finished training at 9 pm, me and the rest of the new lads would have extra duties. These usually involved McClennan going through, in great detail, things we had done wrong the previous week. More often than not it was raining and you could see the rest of the lads looking through the window, sniggering at us thinking, 'Poor sods!'

McClennan also had this habit of using ridiculously long words and sentences. Sometimes you needed the Oxford English Dictionary to work out what he was trying to tell you. Before training, some of the lads used to take advantage of that habit at the team meetings in the old board room. Lads like Huntey, Tea Ropati and George Mann would have a look at the weather outside and if it was bucketing it down they would ask Mike something, knowing full well he could not answer a question in less than ten minutes. It was just any excuse to delay going out onto the training pitch.

The other fad Mike brought in occurred after he had discovered that one of his relatives had apparently lived to something like 103 by taking Royal Jelly supplements. After finding that out he would fetch in these sachets that we were all supposed to take. We were like the kids queuing up for medicine at school, but half of us were sticking them to one side thinking, 'I am not touching that stuff'.

My first eight games at Saints went great; we won the lot and qualified for the Lancashire Cup Final. That was the first competition of the season and was eagerly contested, particularly by Saints and Wigan.

I remember the game vividly because I dropped the first two passes I was given and Wigan's experienced forward Billy McGinty wasted no time in getting into my ear saying words to the effect of 'welcome to the big time'. It was just nerves really – because it was a packed house at Knowsley Road with a crowd of 20,534 jammed in. I had never played in a ground looking as crammed or as noisy as that.

It was a really absorbing game and there were times when we could have won it – but we lost 5–4. If it hadn't been for Shaun Edwards I reckon we would have won because I recall kicking through full-back Joe Lydon's legs a few times and Giz just kept getting back in time and sweeping it up. Although I was pleased with my own performance I was absolutely gutted to lose by a point because we created more chances than them.

Speaking to Wigan and Great Britain prop Andy Platt some time afterwards, he told me I was the talk of the Wigan dressing room. He said, 'We were saying bloody hell, who is this mon?' That was pleasing to hear.

It was one of the first times I got the man of the match in the *Rugby League Express*, although Jason Robinson was Wigan's best player.

After that final the general feeling among the Saints camp was, 'Well they have got a better team than us, they are full-time'. That way of thinking was something the club was trying to get out of. Wigan did have a star-studded international team, but their opponents were going out with a defeated mentality before they had even kicked off.

At the time that team was beginning to think, 'We can do things this year,' having matched them pound for pound in that final.

We had a great pack out that day with a no-nonsense front row of Kevin Ward, Bernard Dwyer and big John Harrison. I packed down with Sonny Nickle in the second row and we had 'Buffer' Forber on the bench.

We had great forwards that year, including big George Mann and Jonathan Neill. The big Cumbrian Jon was one of the toughest blokes I ever played alongside. He might not have won many honours with us, but he was as hard as nails.

At scrum half we had Jonathan Griffiths, a player who I think would do very well in today's game. He was more of a running player, it was like having another forward on. There is a time and place for going yourself and for passing. He never quite got the concept of passing it mind.

As coach, McClennan was influential in bringing over Kiwi three-quarter Jarrod McCracken. McCracken was an up-and-coming player at the time and in 21 games really made an impression at Knowsley Road.

Everybody still talks about that Lancashire Cup Final when he lined up against his big idol Dean Bell. Well, that meant nothing on the day and Jarrod knocked him for six.

We got our revenge over Wigan on Boxing Day when we beat them 41-6 and what a game that was. It was a pretty fierce encounter and even Phil Clarke was rattled and giving penalties away. What a fabulous day – better than any Christmas present. I scored a try and created the first one.

To win games like that with such a convincing score line does wonders for your confidence. Wigan were the best in the business and there was us giving them a caning. It just showed what we were capable of and kept us up there, neck and neck with Wigan, at the top of the table. It was a two-horse race for most of that season, unfortunately we had the odd blip which let us down.

One of those was a dire game that has gone down in St Helens history … a really miserable midweek night at Leigh which cost us the title.

It was an awful night, pouring down rain, sleet, hail, it was windy and the Hilton Park pitch was muddy. I remember playing really well, but Leigh prop Timmy Street ran riot that night. He revelled in the foul conditions, which suited him down to the ground. I had played with Timmy at Oldham and he was as happy as a pig in muck that night and I remember him running the show.

We went out there with all the ability and better players, but the night was that bad we were brought down to their level. It is not an excuse, but it got to the stage where nobody could recognise who was playing for who.

But that game taught me that you have to win games like that if you are going to be a serious title contender. You have to go to Leigh on a foul Wednesday night and come away with two points – not excuses. And we didn't.

Despite that we stayed neck and neck with Wigan that year, level on points and it was always going to come down to that Good Friday game.

There was a massive crowd in Central Park that afternoon – 29,500. We drew 8–8, which was not good enough because Wigan's points difference was better than ours.

I have photographs of that game, but the only thing that sticks in my mind was not losing the title, but the sickening, career ending injury suffered by our prop Kevin Ward.

It was late in the game and Wardy broke his leg badly in the tackle. When I looked over I realised straight away that it was a bad one – it was just horrible.

All I could think was, 'Poor bloke'. He had perhaps another year's rugby left in him, but he was lying there in so much agony. It didn't end for him there either because he had to undergo all kinds of operations on his leg afterwards.

You tend to accept injuries as part and parcel of this game, but ones as bad as that really hit home.

Wardy was a great player and a good bloke too. I didn't really know him properly because I was only the new kid on the block and only played that one season with him. He was a big-framed, gruff Yorkshireman – a real larger than life character who had done the lot at Test level, even winning an Australian Grand Final with Manly.

After games we used to get a case of McEwan's lager and whatever we did not drink, Wardy used to take home with him. Joe Mulcrow was the kit man then and he used to always sort Wardy out with a few extra for when he got home.

In this game you need men like Wardy on your team sheet. In that era especially Wigan used to have it over teams mentally because they had all the stars. But when Wardy's name was on the team sheet opponents would look at it and think, 'Bloody hell, we are up against him tonight'.

When we had our end of the year review, and went through the results we all thought back to Leigh and cursed – that is where we lost it.

There was some satisfaction in the end of season Premiership when we stopped Wigan from winning a grand slam of five cups. The week before that game I was nominated for the Young Player of the Year award, alongside Jason Robinson. We went to a real star-studded bash at the Midland Hotel in the middle of Manchester.

I had enjoyed a really good season, so I was really excited and had to hire a suit for the evening. It was a big night for my girlfriend Andrea also and I arrived there feeling on top of the world. We had been sat down a short while when Maurice Lindsay came up to me and said, 'Well done Chris, at least you were nominated'.

So I knew immediately that I had not won and was really deflated. I thought I had a good chance of winning, being up against Nigel Wright and Jason Robinson. As soon as he said that, after only being there for 10 minutes, it was a real downer. I was disappointed, not just because a lot of people had said that I ought to win that award hands down, but because Lindsay had spoiled what was my biggest evening out. I wanted to enjoy the night thinking, 'I have a great chance of winning this award', but instead I had to sit through the meal knowing I had not won.

That was the week leading up to the Premiership Final, so I had a bit of point to prove. After the season we had had, the club was due some silverware and deserved something more than a couple of runners-up medals. We had come this far – we needed to win something.

Wigan were not taking it easy, and although they were missing a couple of players from their victorious Wembley line-up all they had to do was fetch in a couple more internationals off the bench to replace them. They wanted a clean sweep, make no mistake about that.

It was a really close game, and I remember us having to put in a massive 80-minute defensive stint. Every time I have played at Old Trafford it has been the same. They say the big occasions get to your legs and this was certainly one of them.

The previous year I had played at Old Trafford with Oldham for the Second Division Final and it was half full, but this time it was the main event and was chock-a-block. It was a nerve-racking occasion, and the town was buzzing because we were in a major final. We had a great following there that afternoon.

It was level pegging at the break, after Gary Connolly had grabbed a first half try for us. In the second half two Gus O'Donnell drop goals nudged us in front by a couple of points as the tension mounted. What I really remember more than anything is the sight of Lockers going over for our last try – he fell over the line like a chopped down tree.

I was made up, particularly because I won the Harry Sunderland award for the man of the match. They must have given it for my defensive display, because I didn't make many breaks that day.

I reckon I must have waded through a bit of tackling that day to get the nod, because a lot of the people who write reports and vote for awards only tend to see tries and breaks. You might miss five tackles, but they won't mention that if you score two tries.

The actual Harry Sunderland cup is an old thing, not the most attractive trophy, but it stood proudly on the television set in the front room. All the players who have won the award have their names inscribed on it. I had all these medals I had won at school, St Jude's and St Pat's, then here I was all of a sudden bringing home professional medals.

That Premiership victory was my first professional winner's medal – I think they gave us two crates of Stones Bitter that day for good measure!

In the aftermath of that win there was a real sense that we were not going to carry on playing second fiddle to Wigan – and that was a good feeling. Sadly a lot of that good mood was dashed before the next season – it had started by the selling of our international centre, Gary Connolly, to Wigan of all teams. That to me, even then, made no sense. We had built a good team with good young lads and we were getting there – but then Saints went and sold our best centre!

Gary was our prize asset and the stick and name calling he has had since moving on, and still takes from Saints fans, is unbelievable. Gary knew that his career was rugby league and if somebody offers you probably double what you are getting to move to another club, it would be foolish not to take it.

If Gary Connolly had been offered anywhere near the same deal at Saints as he got at Wigan, I believe he would never have left because he loved it at Knowsley Road.

I look back at those early days at Saints and think of some of the characters rugby league had then – Lockers and Les Quirk were as thick as thieves. They were great players, but they were also puddled and were constantly up to pranks and messing about given half a chance. They used to bring mice to training nights and stick them in our kit bags when we weren't looking. Imagine preparing to go out for a training session and there would be mice running round the dressing room. You'd think, 'What the hell is going on here?'

I got used to that but apparently this was nothing – most of the real jokers had left the club before I came to Knowsley Road, so I can only imagine what that was like.

Having a laugh and joke is harmless enough as long as it does not go too far and get in the way of what you are there for. The trouble nowadays is that if anyone is seen to be having a laugh or is a bit over the top, there is a tendency to mark them out as 'wrong 'uns' and get rid of them. The game has gone too serious in that respect.

I was always able to have a laugh too with the blokes I worked with, and they ensured that I never made the mistake of getting too carried away. If I scored two tries and missed five tackles you could guarantee they would have picked up on the mistakes and would give me plenty of grief the following Monday morning.

I would be on a high after a weekend win and then some big Wigan brickie would turn round and say, 'That Offiah went round you easily enough yesterday, what were you playing at!' But it was doing me more good than harm.

At that stage I was working on sites and homes all round the North-West – I enjoyed it and it kept me fit. I have fond memories now and I could easily slip back into working in a 9 to 5 environment, although probably not plastering. Some players would struggle going to work because they have never known a life other than being professional sportsmen, but I could.

Work teaches you a great deal and during my playing career I had the benefit of sampling both part-time rugby and full-time professionalism under Super League. Although I enjoyed being full-time, that aspect has a down side.

Players today come straight from school and a lot of them have no life skills at all. They don't know what is on the other side of the coin, which can make it difficult for them if things go wrong.

Personally I think for half a day a week the lads should be sent off to work somewhere – say at a sponsor's company – just so they can understand how the other half lives. You can't train all day, five days a week anyway. If the logistics could be worked out, it would benefit the lads, the club and the sponsors.

Rugby league is watched by normal folk who want to be able to chat to players, but we are in danger of moving away from that and more towards the way soccer stars are put on a pedestal.

4

INTO THE LIONS' DEN

Although I had won my first full Great Britain cap against France at Carcassonne in March 1993 I was really looking forward to adding to that.

We had a Test series against the Kiwis to prepare for, and although I had won the Harry Sunderland the year before and had had a good first season at Saints, I did not see myself under any more pressure. I was just enjoying my rugby and I was also working as well, which kept my feet on the ground.

Ahead of that Test series, we did not do much squad training. We went to Catterick army camp with coach Malcolm Reilly and it was a really tough week. The Army recruits who go to Catterick have to complete every discipline and if they fail, they have to go back to the start of their training.

Well, that week we were lined up to do every discipline that they do. What Reilly did when we arrived there was to pair the players up for 'milling'. That is where you stand toe-to-toe and knock seven bells out of one another. That was scheduled for the last day, and I was paired up with Paul Moriarty, Widnes' massive 6ft 4 Welshman.

I was only a kid really so I thought, 'bloody hell', and it was on my mind all week. But I thought, 'Well I'll just have to do it, I will just get stuck in and give it my best shot.' That was hanging over us all week, but during the course of the week, some of the other lads had gone up to Reilly and said, 'I am all right to do the running and the pole carrying, but I can't do the milling!'

Looking back on it, it was a test of character really. Even though I breathed a real sigh of relief on that last day when Reilly said none of us had to do the milling, it stood me in good stead.

Anybody who knows Mal Reilly will know that he is one of the most competitive people you could ever meet. He wants to be as fit as all the lads he is coaching. Even when we have been on tours he always wants to finish first. He would always want to finish the cross-country running ahead of you, and if you did 500 sit-ups, he would do 600. Reilly is exceptional – he has a presence and sets the example to his players by who he was and what he had done as a player. He never took a backward step and he was always superb with me.

During that autumn's Test series I got my first taste of playing at Wembley against the Kiwis. The First Test was played there and turned out to be everything I had ever dreamed of when I had watched it on television or been a spectator.

Our squad stayed in the best hotel and we were treated like kings; from driving in on the team bus, going down Wembley Way, playing and then getting into the baths afterwards it was just fabulous. Over 36,000 fans had travelled down there for the game – and we won, which was the main thing for the series opener.

It was enjoyable because there were some great lads in that side. I was only a kid and the Yorkshire contingent in the pack, particularly, looked after me really well, especially Karl Fairbank and Karl Harrison. Fellow back-rowers Phil Clarke and Denis Betts were perhaps a little less welcoming because they tended to be in Wigan mode, even when they were on international duty.

Even though I knew them all, the Wigan players stuck to their own, although Shaun Edwards was sound with me. I tended to knock about with the Yorkshire lads, like Paul Newlove, who I had first got to know in the previous season's international in Carcassonne.

I was a bit in awe of those Kiwis, because they all appeared so big and I seemed like a midget compared to some of their forwards. Stephen Kearney was roughly the same age as me, but was huge and he tried to give me a crack, but soon realised it was not knocking me off my game.

It is great because I can always look back and say I played with some great players in that series Kelvin Skerrett, Karl Harrison and Karl Fairbank – people who I had admired but as soon as you get to meet them you realise they are good blokes as well.

Gary Schofield was all right as skipper – but the atmosphere in a Great Britain dressing room is pretty quiet, everybody has their own job to do. You don't get people bawling at you do this and do that because everyone is on different territory. You are playing against the best players and teams in the world, so nobody is really comfortable.

The Second Test was at Central Park, Wigan, and we won to clinch the series, which was pleasing because that is where I had played my schoolboy rugby.

We completed the whitewash the following week, but there was no rest for the wicked and the next day I played in the league game against Bradford and came off after about 65 minutes. With international caps, you don't actually get presented with one until you make two appearances. But now I have caps for Great Britain, Ireland, England and Lancashire.

After that series, there was no time for celebrations – we were playing and then it was back in for another normal day at work.

Back with Saints we got off to a bad start at Hull KR's new stadium. The pitch was horrendous, just like a beach – not sand, but mud with bits of shells mixed in with it. Although Hull KR were not the power they once were, they were one of those sides that if you let them play, they would grow a leg.

Our cause was not helped by the sendings off of both Huntey and Sonny Nickle. We also gave plenty of penalties away in a really ill-disciplined performance. Coach Mike McClennan was livid and at half time he stormed into the dressing room to give us what for. There was a table full of drinks and an ice-box. Mike aimed a kick at the ice box, but missed and ended up catching the underside of the sturdy table with his shin and you could see the pain on his face. All the lads in dressing room were creased up, particularly Lockers, but it was a case of keeping your head down so he didn't see you laughing. You could see how much pain he was in, because he was grimacing, limping and he wasn't half shouting.

We missed Gary Connolly, who had gone to Wigan just before the season had started, and Kevin Ward who had retired with that terrible leg injury. Wardy was a big loss because he kind of looked after us and he was a big strike weapon.

The feeling is that life goes on, players will replace the ones that leave. The frustrating thing for me, and I don't know if the others felt the same, was I thought that if I am going to go on and win things I want to be playing with the best players. Gary had gone from Saints to Wigan, and they carried on winning everything.

Some new players came in – Tommy Martyn was the pick of them. He spoke to me prior to coming to Saints and asked what it was like. I just said, 'Just like Oldham, but you are on telly a lot more'. Saints was a club that everybody wanted to come to, but a lot found out they were never the best payers – that is probably why Gary left.

In any professional sport it is all about winning and we had a few dodgy results so Mike came under quite a bit of pressure. We were part-time players though, nobody gave two hoots really about what the coaching situation was. We just turned up on Tuesday and Thursday nights and then on match day.

But Mike had a bit of a side to him and the players used to call him 'Mad Mike'. When he threw ale at that fan at the Warrington game, it was something that we had always expected to happen. It was just a good job it was only a pint of beer beside of him.

He left over the Christmas period after that incident and went back to New Zealand. I was sad to see him go because he was the coach who had given me my start at Saints.

At the end of the day I remember what Paddy Kirwan said to me when I was at Oldham, 'Coaches come and go, but players are forever'. I've never forgotten that. No matter who is running you, the players will still be there, even though the coach may change.

I always use that theory when looking at coaches today. Mike was a good bloke and I have met up with him since. And when Great Britain went on tour to New Zealand I went out for a few pints with him. In fact, I remember on that 1996 tour he could not believe they were playing me on the right side for Great Britain, because I had always played on the left. I think he ended up making a few phone calls to the tour management to say his piece on the matter.

Eric Hughes, who was coaching the Academy at the time, was brought in as McClennan's replacement in January. There are not many coaches available in mid-season. I am not sure whether Hughes was meant to be a stop-gap, but he did a good job for us although we did have a bit of a scratchy season losing eight of our last ten games.

It is hard when you get into a losing streak like that. There is nothing really that the coach can do – it is down to the players to dig themselves out and rally round.

The other aspect of that was we were all on contracts with a system tied to win, lose or draw bonuses. So if we were losing we were all down £300 a week, which is a lot of money.

Experiences like that probably stood me in good stead later in my career – and I have been able to tell the rest of the lads it is down to us when we start losing, the coach can't do everything. I was going through these situations as a young lad, thinking I might have done that differently or handled that in a different way. It was just a case of applying ourselves.

Despite that, we still made it through to the Challenge Cup semi-final after getting the rub of the green with the cup draw playing against Huddersfield, Whitehaven and Doncaster.

That is the beauty of the Challenge Cup – everybody knew that we were not riding as high as we should have been, but we were only 80 minutes from Wembley. However, it was not our year because we came unstuck against an Ellery Hanley inspired Leeds. It just was not happening for us that season – perhaps some of our players had been there too long. It just showed that we could not compete with the likes of Wigan and, to a lesser extent, Leeds, because they were full-time and on good money. And they also had the pick of all the top Australians and Kiwis. On top of that we had all been grafting all week.

However, the good thing Eric Hughes was doing, was bringing in new players at the youth and A team level. We had a lot of lads in the A team who had played too long at that level and were never going to become first teamers, which was not what it was all about. Sometimes it is not a case of people being well liked, you have to be hard and say, 'Player X has been here six years and only played once for the first team, yet there are some young kids who can't get a look in'. It is obvious what needs to happen.

Hughes did that, and although we were not going to be the best

A team the following year, he brought a lot of good young players through. I honestly believe that is what cost him his job ultimately. What Hughes did, was not look after the first team so much as look after the club's future. He had a clear-out and was kind of restructuring the club. He knew from his experience at Widnes as both a player and a coach that this was needed. He has probably taken quite a bit of unfair criticism, but he was good for Saints. He was thinking, 'Let's get a plan in place, let's get a youth structure because we have a load of 27-year-olds in our A team. Let's nurture some kids and bring them through into the first team'.

What he did went unnoticed. But the plan he was putting together was to prove successful.

Eric Hughes was very good for me – and he stood for no nonsense either. Perhaps he even stopped me going off the rails too. I was playing for Great Britain, and perhaps I could have been thinking I have done it all. He used to kick me back on track.

He worked hard on the basics of the game – he was not a Mike McClennan, just a sheer 'hard work, guts and determination' kind of coach. He was also a very quiet coach, but when you talk about hands on, he used to rub us down. It was a case of loosening the muscles up ahead of the warm-up which is important.

We all knuckled down at the end of that season training as hard as we could on the track at Ruskin Drive and in Sherdley Park. Our conditioner at the time was a Scouser, Dave Reid, who was more of an athletics man than a rugby player. We used to try and throw him the ball during tick and pass sessions so that we could smash him with a few proper tackles.

We used to go down the old Bobbies Lane gym with boxing coach John Chisnall, brother of famous Saints players Eric and Dave. It was a fabulous environment to train in to toughen you up, even if it was quite spartan. They had a lot of tough kids there – and I reckon they were not in awe of us, it was probably the other way round.

Boxer Adam Fogerty was playing with us then and you could see that he had hit a bag before. He had been the second best heavy-weight in Britain for a spell. Although he had the legs of a bird, he had the upper body of a Trojan. He was quite a fit bloke, but I suppose you had to be in his game. There was also the advantage of his dad, a famous player in his time, having a pub in Yorkshire. So you can imagine we would stop there for a few pints on the way back from away games across the Pennines!

5

MEETING 'THE CHIEF'

The story so far talks a lot about dreams coming true, and taking on the Aussies in an Ashes Test Series was another one of those being fulfilled. Every kid growing up playing this game ultimately sets their sights on playing against the Kangaroos – testing yourself against the best in the world. It was a fabulous experience, particularly as in those days they only came over here every four years. Great Britain had performed really well the year before in whitewashing the Kiwis, so there was a real air of anticipation in the camp.

Although coach Mal Reilly had dropped a bombshell when he left for Australia to take the Newcastle job, the GB players were really excited at the appointment of Ellery Hanley as his replacement. Ellery was one of my boyhood heroes and although I had played alongside him for England in 1992 and Great Britain against France in 1993, here I was now being coached by him.

Bringing in Hanley on a short-term contract meant the loss of Reilly was not too heavy a blow, and he got the best out of everyone. He had a specific role for me and I was moved up to the front row for the First Test at Wembley. Well, I had not played prop since I was 11 years old. Again it was only Ellery's influence that inspired me, telling me that he had belief in me that I could do the job. He took me to one side and said, 'I want you to play prop for me – you can do it and will do it'. What he was looking for was a high completion rate and quick play-the-balls. If you watch Great Britain's performance, everything was 'concede' and we turned them over in the ruck. That is one of the reasons he had shunted me up to prop and I did the full 80 minutes.

Hanley is a players' man and a professional right out of the top drawer. To have him as coach for that month or so was a fabulous

47

boost. He was no-nonsense, whatever he said had clout, because everyone knew he had done it himself and was still doing it at Leeds.

We respected the bloke with regards to what he wanted to do against the Aussies and his game plan was so simple it was untrue, but it got the result.

The Kangaroos were led by former Saints legend Mal Meninga, on his fourth and final tour to Great Britain. Having been a young lad on that 1982 Invincibles tour, Meninga no doubt wanted to emulate that side and go through Britain unbeaten.

Before the game I was keyed up and bracing myself to taking on the Aussies for the first time, but it could have been worse – at least I didn't have to put up with Cliff Richard, who was doing the pre-match entertainment. Wimbledon yes, but not a rugby league Test match!

The Aussies had a pretty awesome line-up and I was propping against 'The Chief' Paul Harragon. The good thing was because I was so young, I did not give a toss who all these big names were on the team sheet and that probably worked in my favour. Harragon, who I later played alongside at Newcastle, was one tough bloke who always hit you hard, but fair. He only swung his arms if he got really riled.

Obviously they must have been outstanding players to be touring with the Aussies. I look back on it now and think of their pack that day: Ian Roberts, Steve Walters, Paul Harragon, Paul Sironen, Bradley Clyde and Brad Fittler, not a bad set of forwards, that.

That First Test was an unbelievable triumph, particularly because we lost skipper Shaun Edwards early on when he was sent off for a high tackle on Bradley Clyde. There were only 25 minutes on the clock when Giz got his marching orders and we just looked at each other and muttered 'bloody hell' and shook our heads. It is hard enough beating the mighty Australians at 13-a-side, never mind when you are a man down. Giz was also the one man in our key pivotal role at scrum half. Over my career I have found that you sometimes have your best games and wins when you have 12 players on the park. I am not suggesting it is an advantage starting with 12, but sometimes losing a man can just lift the rest of the lads that extra few per cent to get you through.

No matter what the sport or competition is, it is so important to get a good start. We knew that and the Aussies knew that, that is why it is really annoying when you get one or two cynics suggesting that the 'Roos deliberately took it easy in the First Test just to ensure sell-out crowds for the following matches in the series. It is not in the Aussies nature to give you anything, so all that talk was complete rubbish.

It was one hell of a game and we won it with sheer grit and determination. It was a real against-the-odds triumph.

Jonathan Davies grabbed our only try that day, what an absolute belter it was too. The Welshman left their full-back Brett Mullins, who was no slouch, grabbing at fresh air before touching down in the corner.

That image was beamed everywhere and every time that I see that picture or the clips of that on television now I think I was part of that great achievement. I know I might not have scored the winning try but I made a big contribution to the win.

We were all shattered as the game reached its closing stages, and it was unbelievably draining. When Steve Renouf scored for them to peg it back to 6–4 with nine minutes to go, it was a case of we have come this far we have to hang on in there. At that time as well we were on £4,000 a man to win, so that gives you a bit more incentive to hang in there.

One good thing about going to Wembley in 1994 was that I had been the year before against the Kiwis, so I was not nervous about it being a new place and experience. I knew my role and how to approach it. It was more enjoyable also because I had already played there.

Throughout my career, whether at Whitehaven, Wakefield or Wigan I always sat in the same spot. I am not sure if it is Feng Shui or what but the spot I first pick when I walk into a room is the one I stick with. It is not superstition, just something I sense when I go somewhere new so I know where I am going to change. Kit man Stan Wall knows the way I work and it used to wind me up if he stuck me in a corner, with numbers 10 and 12 at the side of me. If you are crammed into a corner under the stand at somewhere like

Salford changing on a little chair with no room to move, you think, 'what's going on?'

Although it was great to take that First Test, and it was the first time I had ever played in a winning side against the Aussies, it does not take a rocket scientist to know that we had achieved nothing. We had been to Stringfellow's and partied on into the early hours in London with our four grand burning a hole in our pockets and feeling like two bob millionaires. But once the champagne bubbles had gone flat you think, 'We have two more games left here'. We had won nothing yet, but were thinking, 'How good will it be if we win the next test to take the Ashes for the first time since 1970?'

The Aussies have a great winning mentality, and that is something I have always aspired to. I don't like losing at anything, more so at rugby – something I am competent at doing. I am not the best golfer in the world, but if I am out there on the course I hate losing there too. That is the mentality needed to succeed and something the British nation as a whole needs. Everybody mentions the Aussies and how good a sporting nation they are, but they are no fitter or stronger than we are. It is just down to their country's attitude, belief and confidence.

As far as I am concerned there is too much tolerance and acceptance of losers in British sport. I would not want any praise for coming second. At the end of the day, if you lose you should hang your head and ask yourself why you have lost again.

There is a saying, 'Britain loves a loser' – just look at the affection for Frank Bruno and Eddie 'the Eagle' Edwards. That is what is wrong with our country, we can take second best where the Aussies can't and the sooner we can get into that mentality we might start competing again as a sporting nation.

Looking back on that series now, I think our biggest problem was that our tactics did not change from the First Test, to the Second and to the Third. The Australians corrected their weaknesses and changed their tactics accordingly, and because we did not alter our game, they knew what was coming and were ready for it and knew how to combat it.

The Aussies have not lost the Ashes in this country since 1959. We knew it was going to be a tough task to grab them at Old Trafford. A crowd of 44,000 packed into the 'Theatre of Dreams' in anticipation, geed up by the Wembley victory. It just did not happen for us, they simply took us apart, beating us 38–8 and I came off after an hour. The media had really built us up so much after the First Test and in the run-up to the Second, then a few days after the defeat they were all writing us off. When we picked up the papers and read the slating we were getting, it sowed elements of doubt in our minds.

For the deciding test at Elland Road, Ellery moved me back to loose forward and put Phil Clarke at stand-off, but unfortunately we picked up a few early injuries. Alan Hunte limped off and Clarke went off early, and we just crumbled.

After that it was back to league rugby – three days after that final test I was playing at Doncaster in mid-week. Old Trafford and Wembley one week – Tattersfield the next!

I did not really get time to reflect on the Test Series – in fact I was back at work on the Monday, the day after that final test defeat and they gave me plenty of stick, with welcoming words like, 'What about you shower!' It made sure my feet were well and truly planted on the ground.

Saints had gone out and spent some money in the summer, bringing in Scott Gibbs and Apollo Perelini from rugby union and Bobbie Goulding from Widnes.

It was good that the club were spending money, but they did not really know what they were getting in two out of three of those signings. Bringing the rugby union players in was a massive gamble. It was a case of what have we got today, and in Scott and Apollo it was two converts hoping to make a mark on the game as early as possible.

The two union lads arrived in the summer and had a pre-season with us running on the cinder track at Ruskin Drive. I trained with Apollo, and we put one another through it on the track. I was surprised how fit he was for such a big bloke. Those were the days when you used to get hundreds watching training. So when you were sprinting there was always that bit more competition between the lads because there were 300 people watching. We always had a forwards group and a backs group and as the season drew nearer we would go into individual positions, as in wingers sprinting with wingers, props with props and back row together.

I always kept something back during sprints, kind of going through the motions to keep a bit in the tank. I don't play like that, but used to say, 'Never bet on me scoring the first try, always put me down for the last one!'

When Gibbsy came he was a big name in rugby union, but he was so unfit it was frightening. In his first sessions, he was a lap behind all the forwards, so you can imagine what we were thinking. This chap had a big reputation, a great Welsh player of renown but he was so far off the pace in those first couple of sessions.

One thing with Gibbsy was he took a massive gamble crossing the divide and coming to league. He knew what he had to do to cut it in our game. After that he trimmed down, had a different physique on him and became one of the best trainers at the club. If I speak of Scott Gibbs now I think of a bloke who I hold in high esteem. He played with his heart, playing and running at 100 miles an hour. Nobody could question his commitment to Saints – a tremendous player.

He and Goulding made their debuts in that first league game of the season. Saints started disastrously, losing our opening game at home to newly promoted Doncaster 30–29. It was a massive shock because Doncaster had never beaten Saints before so it was a piece of history I was not happy to be part of.

I recall the game because Doncaster's South African full-back, Jamie Bloem, ran riot that afternoon. He was fending six men off, side-stepping four more and he scored two tries. I remember going home and my dad, who very rarely mentions rugby to me said, 'You want to start running like that Bloem!' At the end of November, Bloem was banned for taking steroids.

Still Doncaster had that win and you can't take it away from them. The number of programmes that were sent over from Doncaster for the Saints players to sign was unbelievable. You would have thought they had won the Challenge Cup. It was the same when we went there, with a load of Donny speccies bringing that same programme of the time their side beat the Saints for us to autograph. Burly centre Vila Matautia played and scored for Donny in that opening game and he signed for us later in the season as an impact player.

We recovered and put together some decent wins and then we nearly ended up getting knocked out of the Regal Trophy on a dreadful afternoon at Batley. Their ground is called Mount Pleasant, but there was nothing pleasant about that pitch with that big slope, particularly as it was ankle deep in mud that afternoon.

I had never played there before but it was a bit like Dewsbury's Crown Flatt, where I had played the previous year. That time I recall Mike McClennan saying, 'I am playing you sub today, you decide – first half or second half'. I remember thinking to myself then that I would rather wait for the toss because I didn't fancy running up that hill in all that mud. Typically I ended up coming on in the second half playing up the hill.

On this occasion against Batley, I played in the first half – uphill – and it didn't work out because I ended up getting a bang to the back and coming off at half time.

We were lucky that afternoon and only just scraped a draw, with Dave Lyon grabbing a try in the last minute. We won the replay easily enough at Knowsley Road, but once again Wigan blocked our progress in that trophy and they just edged us 24–22 at Central Park.

It was a pretty decent season for us, apart from an iffy spell in the winter and then we took on Wigan in the Challenge Cup.

That was one hell of a game. As I have said before, they had the best players money could buy and their side that day was: Henry Paul; Jason Robinson, Inga Tuigamala, Gary Connolly, Martin Offiah; Frano Botica, Shaun Edwards; Kelvin Skerrett, Martin Hall, Neil Cowie, Denis Betts, Mick Cassidy, Phil Clarke. Paul Atcheson and Andy Farrell were on the bench. All internationals!

But Eric Hughes was building a side, slotting the pieces into place. Our line-up that day was Steve Prescott; Alan Hunte, Scott Gibbs, Dave Lyon, Anthony Sullivan; Phil Veivers, Bobbie Goulding; Jonathan Neill, Keiron Cunningham, Ian Pickavance, Chris Joynt, Sonny Nickle, Shane Cooper. Subs were Mark Elia and Andy Dannatt.

We were desperately unlucky, threw everything at them and Ian Pickavance's drop goal got us the draw which was unusual because he was possibly the worst kicker I have ever seen.

Our replay at Knowsley Road drew a massive crowd and because the Republic of Ireland v England football match was abandoned due to English fans rioting at Lansdowne Road our game got top billing on BBC1's *Sportsnight* that evening. And rightly so too!

Unfortunately we were so drained from throwing absolutely everything into that Saturday game that we had nothing left for the replay. Wigan v Saints games are always really intense – they do drain you.

Again Wigan had the advantage of being full-time players, while our lads had all been back to work on the Monday, Tuesday and Wednesday, so when it came to the second hit, we just lacked the ammunition. I had only finished work at 4 pm that day, so I had to leg it home and put a tracksuit on and headed straight back out. I scored a try that night but Wigan were always in the driving seat and won 40–24, which was on the cards pretty early on.

You can tell more or less how a game is going to go after about 15–20 minutes. You can assess players' attitudes and whether the little things are being done right. You can always rescue games, but it is only the players who can do that. I probably didn't really think on those lines back in 1995 mind, you learn as you get older.

Wigan always had legendary teams in the early 90s and that team went on to win the Challenge Cup for the eighth time in succession.

That must have been 'Inga the winger' Tuigamala's first season at Central Park. I always enjoyed playing against people who had come over from union to try their hand at league. More so people like huge former All Black Tuigamala – I always tried to hit him harder, especially as he was so big. I don't know what it is whether it is their reputation or the fact you want to prove our game is harder.

Earlier I recall playing for Oldham A team against Jonathan Davies, a player who came over with a massive reputation from rugby union when he joined Widnes in 1989. I chased him around the pitch throughout the game thinking at the time if my career ended that day at least I got one big shot on him.

Union players who come over have a hell of a lot of respect for league because you have to be a lot fitter. In our game you can have all the necessary physical attributes, but it is a case of still having those when you are up and back times six for every set. If somebody makes ten tackles one after the other, there is no way that tenth tackle will be as hard as the first one. Some people don't realise how tough the game is and some of the games are lightning quick. Playing at club level is quick but when you go up to international it is like playing on skates because it is so much quicker. The Under-21s say the same when they come through to play Super League.

Our season that year finished with a bit of a damp squib, getting knocked out of the Premiership trophy at Headingley, despite leading 20–6 at half time. Leeds also had Gary Schofield sent off for abusing the referee. We had finished fourth in the league, won nothing, but you could see that the foundations were being put into place for the future. You could see Eric Hughes' plan beginning to work. All of a sudden you were seeing players six months to a year earlier than you would have done in another coaching era.

On a sadder note my old mate Gus O'Donnell developed kidney trouble and had to pack in. Ducky went to the same school as me and we grew up together, rugby-wise. He signed for Wigan at 17, when I was training with Wigan as a 16-year-old. It was always nice to have some faces who you can recognise and Ducky was one of those. In years to come we ended up playing for the same team at Saints, something we hadn't done since playing for St John Fisher.

It was sad that illness forced him out of rugby league, because he was a fierce competitor. He still is – we still enjoy a game of golf together, so he has been on the road to recovery a good while. It has probably done him some good not playing because he will be fit in himself – he's now a fitness instructor but I bet he does not feel half as stiff when he gets up in the morning as I do.

6

A PAWN IN RUGBY LEAGUE'S WAR

When *News International* slapped their proposals for a new Super League and a significant amount of cash onto the table it sent shock waves throughout the game.

There had already been a lot of talk among the players about what had already kicked off in Australia, where the ARL had been approaching English players to go Down Under.

I had been due to meet representatives from the ARL, but on the day of my appointment I got a phone call from Saints. They said, 'It is nothing to worry about, just come up'.

When I got up to the club, there were four or five of the other players who had also been earmarked for a Super League deal. We looked at each other shrugging our shoulders, but when we got into the boardroom there were board members, representatives and solicitors. It was all pretty intimidating stuff. The board told me that the club was thinking of going into the proposed new Super League and they wanted me to commit to signing up to it. I was a little naive and I told them I had a meeting with the ARL later that day. Their ears pricked up once they heard that and all of a sudden they started talking money and wanted me to sign on the dotted line. So I signed a contract and received £100,000 thrown in as a loyalty bonus to go into Super League. They gave me a cheque there and then. I thought, 'This is unbelievable getting this money for nothing really.' I probably didn't realise how much it really was at the time.

I didn't end up going to that meeting with the ARL because I was happy as Larry with the deal I'd just signed.

At that time all the players were in the same boat, and we were just going with the flow just assuming that the clubs would make all the decisions. But then all of a sudden it became like a turf war and the other players, who had not been called in, knew that probably five or six of us had been given loyalty bonuses. There was even talk that the rest of the squad would sign up to the ARL to throw a spanner in the works. But that all came to nothing because the problem was headed off and in the end they all got their wages doubled or trebled, so it was happy days all round. Everybody received a new full-time contract, and when you get a deal like that you soon learn to keep quiet.

With hindsight, all this influx of television cash was something that went out of control and won't come round again. I just count my blessings that I was very fortunate to be there at the right time when that big money was slapped on the table. And as an up-and-coming international player, just getting to the top of my game I was able to take advantage of that.

I think the whole thing snowballed out of control – and to this day I still think that when I walked into that room even the club did not know what it was doing. If the Super League and its clubs had its time all over again it would actually sit down and think, 'Whoa! Let's not make any rash decisions. We can't be doubling everybody's wages'.

I think it was panic stations all round. The RFL was paranoid about losing the best British talent to Australia. The clubs were probably under pressure too – somebody was in their ears saying, 'Make sure you keep hold of players X, Y and Z'.

And the players who had not been given loyalty payments also had to be kept sweet. I was just a pawn in the game, with two rival Aussie television broadcasters fighting over my signature.

When you go down to the bare bones of it, it was television companies who wanted rights to show rugby league in Great Britain and Australia. A lot of money was spent over the wrangling and loyalty payments and the like. But that is all by the by now – some British players signed up to the ARL but they had already done what they wanted to do.

The clubs will look back on that period and kick themselves. Apart from the big successes, there have also been losers and victims and my former club Oldham was one of those first casualties, although they are still plugging away in the town.

You could never knock the players for taking the money, but the clubs were given the cash and how that was distributed was up to them. The clubs knew they could easily lose their players, so that is why they trebled wages in some cases.

Although the game needed the television company and the money that came with it, it also needed a bunch of individuals coming up with a business plan. The clubs seemed to have no business plan, it was all just a case of, 'It is burning a hole in my pocket, let's get it spent!'

The average wage then was probably £10–£15,000, because most of the lads were manual workers. All of a sudden they were making a few bob playing so work ceased to be a problem. There were obviously some lads like Dave Lyon, who had worked his way up through with his job at Wigan Council, who was not prepared to give up his job for his last couple of years in the game. That was the end of Dave, but he has probably had the last laugh.

The wrangling became a major distraction during my spell Down Under in the summer of 1995. Newcastle Knights' coach Mal Reilly had approached me earlier in the season with a view to spending the off-season in Australia and I jumped at the chance. I flew straight over to Australia at the end of Saints' season in 1994–95 and teamed up with the Knights.

Newcastle were one of the clubs who had signed up to the ARL, so when I talk about being a pawn, all of a sudden I was one over there in the thick of it. I had an opportunity to sign a three-year deal with Newcastle which came at one of the most intimidating meetings I have ever had. They wanted me to switch my allegiance from Super League and sign ARL with Newcastle. It was a meeting at the Manly Pacific Hotel between Bob Fulton, Mal Reilly and myself and they told me to give Super League their money back and sign for the Knights. It was more money but I didn't know what to do.

It was a really intimidating meeting – frightening as anything because they were two men I highly respected. I am not saying they were being pushy; it was more a case of them being shovey.

They told me to go away and think about it. With all the figures going through my head, it felt like walking on a knife edge. I had only gone there for an off-season! Some players had signed Super League and switched their allegiances, but they had to go to court with their cases. At this meeting Fulton kept quoting players who had switched back and said they had lawyers in place, so it would not be a problem for me. But I thought, 'I don't want to be doing that – I have only come out for a game of rugby'.

Things were hotting up and St Helens knew what Newcastle were trying to do so Mally Kay used to phone me up regularly because of the talk of me not coming home. The thing that scared me off was I was over there on my own and I didn't want to be fighting any legal battles. These were uncharted waters for me and there had not really been one big swap by then, so it could not have been as easy as they were making out.

I played about ten games for the Knights in the Winfield Cup. Unfortunately, because I needed to have my knee fixed when I first got there it was a month before I got fit and started playing again. On my first touch of the ball I scored against St George. Again that was great. You could not have written a better script. I was playing alongside some superb players like Joey Johns and Paul Harragon, the Chief.

The Chief, who I talked about earlier, was immense. I remember him in one really tough game against Manly at the Marathon Stadium having a real tussle with Spud Carroll. They were at each other all game and then Knights kicked off straight to Carroll who steamed onto the ball. The Chief had started sprinting for him as soon as they kicked off and they both tupped each other's heads and were carted off.

The Chief was a gentleman off the field – but he was also a legend over there. It was only while I was over there, seeing his face plastered over the back of buses, that I realised how big a sporting icon he was Down Under.

The training was an eye-opener, they had different types of training machines such as the gauntlet, which is like a big massive cage with rubber prongs in it. You have to take the ball and run through it and the prongs would hit you on the arms and legs. If you didn't go through it full belt it hit you like you were being whipped.

I enjoyed it all and that was the first time I had really got into some serious weight training. Even though I was full-time, the majority of the Aussies I was playing alongside were working as well. A few of them still work now.

When you were tackled they used to sledge you with all kinds of stuff. It was sticks and stones and the tackles didn't hurt any more than over here. All that stuff is a load of rubbish about them being fitter and stronger. I can argue with anybody on that because I have been there and played it.

I loved being there, it was such a great lifestyle and environment. My girlfriend Andrea came over and joined me for three weeks while I was over there. I lived next door to a World Champion surfer – I didn't even know who he was. Former Hull, Sheffield and GB hooker Lee Jackson was also over there playing at South Sydney at the time and he used to come up and see me with his family. It was a great place to be.

The build-up to games was like our football games in Britain. They were special days out and it was a big thing in Newcastle, with crowds of about 17,000. It's almost a national sport there, everybody spoke to you as you walked down the street.

They are rugby mad. Newcastle were sponsored by a company called Stockland, who owned the big shopping malls over in Australia. Every Thursday we had to go to the supermarket and meet the fans and we would be there for two hours signing autographs for thousands of people.

Being a rugby league player over there was probably like being Alan Shearer or Michael Owen in England. You could not go out anywhere without getting stopped by fans.

There were a lot of British lads over at the time: Lee Jackson, Jonathan Davies, Andy Platt, Phil Clarke, Allan Bateman and Gary Connolly but most of them had signed for the ARL.

I was there for four months in total and I was under massive pressure to stay there because I was having a good season. I was back on song recovering from my knee injury, but I was under the sort of intense pressure that I didn't really need. I was just there to play rugby and progress in my career. This was supposed to be part of my learning curve as a player and I could have done without all the earache I was getting off the pitch.

Saints were on to Newcastle to get me home and they started legal proceedings to get me back. So reluctantly I came home. At the time I just did not know what to do – I was in limbo. Saints wanted me back safely home out of harm's way, especially as the 1995 season had started creeping up, but I wanted to stay at Newcastle and play in the play-offs.

Maurice Lindsay was over at the time in his capacity as the Super League Chief Executive and he phoned me at my home in Australia. He said, 'What we'll do is send a car for you at night and get you out of there'.

But I told him I didn't want to sneak out and that I could leave Newcastle with my head held high because I had done a good stint for them. I just wanted advice on what to do, but all he kept going on about was sending a car round at the dead of night.

After that John Ribot, who was one of Super League's top men in Australia, used to phone me and eventually it was resolved. When I went to pick my plane ticket up, there was a nice envelope waiting for me at the airport. But full credit to Mal Reilly – he let me make my own decision.

I still have plenty of friends in Newcastle and I gave 110 per cent for them. I didn't really put a foot wrong there, although it would have been nice to play in those play-offs.

Before I came back home I went and had a week up in Yenda, where I had played some years previously in my Oldham days.

That experience taught me so many things in life. And I really enjoyed playing – even though I was trying to beat the clock with my injury early on.

In a way I regret not signing up at Newcastle for three years – I would have loved that. But whenever I start thinking of that, I always remind myself that I would not have won those first two Challenge Cup medals at Wembley and that first ever Super League trophy. At the time we didn't really know that Saints were on the threshold of such success. Saints had looked after me, and I was happy with what they had given me with regards to my contract.

When I arrived back at Knowsley Road for the start of the 1995 Centenary season, I could not help but keep thinking about

Newcastle. Missing out on the Australian Grand Final series play-offs was never far from my thoughts. I kept thinking I could have been part of that, particularly as the Knights went as far as the final eliminator before losing to Manly.

I think you could even say I was a bit resentful about having to return, but still St Helens were my employers and it was right that they had first pick on my services.

7

A GAME IN TRANSITION

After returning from Australia, I was straight back into the thick of the action at Saints without any pre-season build-up. I was match hardened though, and the only thing I really missed back here was a few hard training sessions.

Nevertheless, the stint was good for my development, although I know the board and my coach had mixed feelings about me going Down Under. Eric Hughes tried to push me away from going – he had played over there himself in the 1970s. He believed I risked meltdown through playing 'too much rugby'. In that era we had other cup competitions, so you were playing 40-odd games a year and that is why Hughesy had tried to talk me out of it.

But it was all done now and once I stopped moping about Newcastle, I started looking forward to the year ahead. On the plus side my knee was sorted and I was match fit. I didn't feel fatigued then, maybe it only caught up with me a few more years down the line because when you tot it up I went from the start of 1994 all the way through to the end of 1996 playing back-to-back rugby.

There were times in that year when I did feel tired, but because we were now full-time we had more time to relax and recover.

The 1995 season was a bit of a stop-gap one – the last winter season before Super League. We wore an unusual blue and white striped kit to mark the centenary season in Saints' original colours. But I thought it was an awful kit really, having always been used to red and white.

It was quite a disjointed short season and unusually we played Wigan in the last week of August and were hammered. There were a few lop-sided scores dished out that year, including plenty by us. It was like a points bonanza, putting 55 on Bradford, 66 on

Workington, 62 on Sheffield, 50 on London and 58 on Halifax.

For the players it was more like a honeymoon period – we were all on better money and looking forward to the new competition starting in the summer. Having said that, the season was all over the shop. Nobody could really adjust to the format, particularly as the season stopped after two months to accommodate the World Cup.

It seemed bizarre to stop when we were in full flow that way. The lads who were not on international duty got an extended month's holiday, while the rest of us were at it hammer and tongs at the highest level.

The organisation of the World Cup itself went quite smoothly and raised the profile of our game immensely – but it did seem a mad time to have it.

The World Cup seemed to be like the icing on the cake to our game – it looked as though we were at last getting somewhere in organising a massive international competition. The tournament had the fans flocking in their droves and there was a feel-good factor there too.

England kicked off the tournament with a Group A game against Australia at Wembley. More than a few cynics argued that this was to help set up a repeat match in the Final, which was also at Wembley – and that would guarantee another bumper crowd. Playing them in the group stage meant we could not be drawn against each other in the semis.

With what was going on in the world of rugby league with the creation of Super League, there was added pressure for England to do well.

Anyway we won that first game against the Aussies and I came off the bench and scored. After chipping through, I just managed to get my hands onto the greasy ball. When I touched down, the ball squirted up so it looked like I had not grounded it properly. I definitely grounded it – only just mind – but Keith Leyland was the in-goal judge that day. Well Keith was a Wigan bloke, who used to referee us as kids so as soon as he gave me the wink, I knew it was going to be given.

I did not play in England's midweek game against Fiji, but there were 26,000 fans packed into Central Park for that. It was an amazing figure given they struggled to get that for Test matches against the Aussies in later years.

Over 14,000 filed into Headingley for the group match against South Africa – not the best opposition in the world by any stroke of the imagination.

The score finished up at 46–0 and it was quite a different line-up from the side that played in the opener at Wembley. I played left-sided back row that night, with Martin Offiah as the left winger.

At Saints I was very much used to having my winger Anthony Sullivan stopping on his chalk – so I always knew where to find him. If I broke down the wing, I always knew Sully would be on his touchline waiting for the pass. It was like second nature at Knowsley Road.

But for England that night, because there was so much space opening up in the middle, Offiah kept coming inside looking for the ball. As a result I broke through a few times but ended up throwing about three pearling passes at the touch judge that night, just expecting the winger to still be there. It just showed the limited time England had had together as a squad and we did not really know each other's style of play.

It was kind of a frustrating tournament for me because I only started one game and was on the bench for two more, including the final. I had gone down to the World Cup Final at Wembley as a spectator in 1992 and remember thinking to myself when I was watching Kevin Ward slugging it out, how good must it be to play in a World Cup Final. It was disappointing to lose my starting spot in the second row, particularly as I had done well in the previous two Test Series against New Zealand and Australia.

The back row for both the opener and the final was the Wigan trio of Phil Clarke, Denis Betts and Andrew Farrell.

I don't know what it was but I never really got on with Phil Larder that well. He had been around the Great Britain squad before, but only as an assistant to Malcolm Reilly. I respected Malcolm because of what he had done at the highest level but I just didn't hit it off with Phil. We did not see eye to eye on a number of things, although I also don't doubt that he was under pressure to accommodate Farrell, Clarke and Betts. Faz is a great player, but he was not doing anything I was not doing. Still his was the name up in lights at the time.

It was difficult playing off the bench, because I had never really been a sub in my career. Out of my long career I reckon it only adds up to about 20 times, which is not that many out of 400-odd games. I always found it hard to play substitute, particularly back in 1995 because it was a 13-man game – not the 17-man game we have now. As a result of that you did not know when or if you would be coming on. Substitutions were not as tactical then, it was a case of, 'We have got our best 13 and this is how we will play'.

I came on 11 minutes from the end, just after Andrew Johns had scored the match-winning try. It was too late for me to have any impact on the game and that was disappointing. Although I had the honour of playing in a World Cup Final, thoughts did cross my mind that I would have been better off sitting in the stands for the contribution I made that afternoon.

There is a disappointment at being a substitute, even in 2003 and 2004 when I was picked on the bench I was always bitterly disappointed. I took that as a weakness in my game and thought to myself, 'If I can't command a starting spot, I'm not the best second row here!'

Immediately after the World Cup it was straight back into league football and even though Wigan were running away with the title, we kept plugging away. I never viewed any game or tournament as lost – every game I played I felt we had to win.

There had been quite a bit of movement on the transfer front with Saints buying international centre Paul Newlove from Bradford for a record fee made up of £250,000 plus Paul Loughlin, Bernard Dwyer and Sonny Nickle.

At the time I had mixed feelings really, on one hand I was disappointed because Lockers, Bernard and Sonny had kind of looked after me at Saints and were always good pros to have in your team. All of a sudden three good lads were going, but Saints were thinking of the bigger picture and putting a last piece in the jigsaw. Maybe those three did not figure in it. That was sad, but Bradford got some good years out of those players, and Sonny even ended up returning to give Saints a few good years back at

Knowsley Road.

I knew nothing about what was going on behind the scenes. It was quite sad though when you think Lockers could have gone to Wigan in the late 80s, just like Gary Connolly did, and helped himself to a drawer-full of medals there. He was so loyal – even though he was from Garswood, he was St Helens through and through. So was Bernard – if you cut those two in half you will find they are pure red and white of the Saints.

To be told, all of a sudden, that they had to leave the club they had supported and played for since they were colts was like cutting their arms and legs off. You hear tales that they both had tears in their eyes when they were told. Even now you can understand how gutted they must have been.

On the other hand the mere fact that we were buying players of the calibre of a prolific try scorer like Newy was good sign for the health of the club. Newy was a world class centre and really fitted the bill. Chief executive David Howes milked the publicity for all it was worth, delivering him to the press conference in a Securicor van.

I struck up a great rapport with Newy in the years that followed and people always talk about how deadly the left flank partnership was between Tommy Martyn, myself, Newy and Sully. If the four of us were to sit down in years to come we would probably just talk about how well we complemented each other and how deadly a partnership we had down the left.

We played to it that much that opposing teams were obviously aware of it, and made plans to nullify it. But they just could not stop us – which is a good job really because we didn't have much else in the way of a game plan. Opposing coaches used to stack their defence to the right when they played Saints – there was always an abundance of tacklers in front of us but we always had a bag of tricks to get past them.

Off the field, David Howes had joined the club and he had brought some fresh thinking with him. He had a proven record in the administration side of the game and was good at organising things, although, I think at times he thought he was the chief executive of Manchester United, not St Helens. He had such big plans and even years after he had left, the lads who played under his time joked about some of those schemes. We used to have meetings in the clubhouse, and he would say things like, 'See where you are sitting now, this is going to be an Italian restaurant'. He had a real vision to transform the Knowsley Road ground. You can't knock him for that and for being enthusiastic.

Howes also pioneered Saints' push into the city of Liverpool. We played a couple of games at Anfield, which was a fantastic experience and a real privilege, especially as I am a Liverpool FC fan. We all touched the 'This is Anfield' sign as we ran out, which was a really good feeling.

Prior to one of those games I was part of the publicity drive, which involved being sent into the Liverpool schools to spread the word. Vila Matautia, Andy Northey and myself visited one school and I knew we were going to be up against it because the kids thought Vila was John Barnes! We knew it was going to be tough breaking into Liverpool after that experience. Sporting cultures are different from town to town and loyalties run deep. It is like telling a Whitehaven fan that they should merge with Workington.

The Liverpool experiment was a case of Howes spotting a soccer-mad city of a half a million people, which is only nine miles up the road. He wanted to persuade some of them to convert to our game in the summer. It is a way of thinking that still has currency at Saints today and we did a lot more missionary work in Liverpool in 2004. There is a lot of untapped spectator potential in Liverpool, but it is one of those things – they are soccer mad and rugby league does not seem to register much in terms of interest.

Our Regal Trophy run was quite a good aspect of 1995–96, starting with our opening round at Keighley. The unfashionable Yorkshire side were buzzing at that time on a tide of 'Cougarmania' – and that was enough to entice the BBC television cameras to the match. England coach Phil Larder was in charge and they had bought some pretty useful players. They were keen to press their claims for inclusion in the Super League – they certainly made an effort off the field, with Lawkholme Lane becoming Cougar Park and their fans making a bit of a din. There was nothing glamorous about the place when the rain sheeted down. But we were never in trouble and had a 20–4 lead at the break, eventually winning

42–14 with both Scott Gibbs and me bagging a couple of tries each.

We had to rely on a couple of late tries to see off Hull at the Boulevard in the next round and then we thumped Halifax in the quarter-finals.

In the semi-final we put an unheard-of 80 points past Warrington – a result which finished off their coach Brian Johnson. Results like that are no good really – even as a player you don't get much out of that sort of kick off and score, kick off and score routine. I am sure some of our speccies liked it though, particularly as it was a local derby. Warrington had a decent team that night, but they had kind of given up. Saints just showed what they could do when they turned it on – we could run riot. Four days later we put 54 points past them, this time in the league.

We were just happy to get to the Regal Trophy Final. The competition had been around since 1971 and the switch to summer meant this was going to be the last ever one. Saints had not had the best of fortune in that competition, only winning it the once back in 1988.

We were confident facing Wigan, despite them boasting all the star names. Huddersfield's McAlpine Stadium was a relatively new venue on the rugby league circuit and there was a big 17,590 crowd packed inside, generating a great atmosphere.

There was a good vibe among both players and fans, this was not going to be one of those mismatches from the late 80s. Wigan skipper Shaun Edwards was even going round saying Saints should start as favourites on account of our drubbing of Warrington in the semi. That was probably a bit of reverse psychology to transfer some of the expectation and pressure onto us.

It made for an absolutely fantastic finale to that competition and I suppose winter rugby league.

For me personally, however, the build-up was not brilliant. I had ruptured the AC joint in my shoulder against Oldham at Knowsley Road on 13 December. I did not play for a month and my first game back was the Regal Trophy Final, not the easiest way to ease back in! Bar a few bangs and bumps, it was probably the first real injury that I had had. It did have an effect on me in that final because I missed the first two tackles of the game and probably should not have come back so soon. But it was a major final – and I had not played in that many up until then.

We were very unlucky to lose that game – with a little bit of individual brilliance and inspiration from Henry Paul and Jason Robinson making a difference. Paul grabbed a couple of tries that afternoon – I really think he was the biggest difference between two good sides that day.

The game could have gone either way and we led at half time with Joey Hayes and Paul Newlove going over for tries to cancel out an early one by Inga Tuigamala. Wigan had their share of luck, mind you, particularly when Scott Gibbs tried to clear his line only to lose the ball on the try line to present a soft try for Kris Radlinski. Then Paul zipped in for a real dazzler of a try – but we kept on battling, with Keiron Cunningham stretching through a heap of bodies to touch down. We only trailed 19–16 and then Paul nipped in for the clincher. It was not Gibbsy's afternoon – he was sent off in the last minute for leading into a tackler with his elbow.

We were all desperately disappointed to go so close and lose. We were gutted really and kept thinking, 'We should have won that game'. We had the chances to win that day but it just did not happen.

On the positive side we knew our day was coming. There was a real consolation in our own belief that this side of ours was ready to kick on and win things. The gap was clearly closing between Wigan and us. Some of the lads we had fast-tracked were probably 18 months ahead of themselves. Maybe that Centenary season helped blood them and gave them a year in the first team that they would not have had in a regular season. It probably helped them mature into the good players they became. Added to that we had a nucleus of quality players who were in the pomp of their career.

In one sense it was the side that Eric Hughes built, but he was given his cards as we stood on the threshold of big things and was replaced by Aussie coach Shaun McCrae.

When I was away on international duty I recall David Howes being quite friendly with Shaun McCrae and he had got him to come up and do some sessions alongside Eric Hughes at the club. McCrae was already over here for the World Cup and came up and took the odd session at the ground, so the seed must have been planted then. It came to fruition shortly afterwards when he replaced Hughes as head coach.

I was sad to see Hughes go – he paid the price for restructuring the club. Hughes probably made the club what it was in that era.

It is hard not to let a player or coach's departure not affect your outlook and the way you react to those who replace them. Looking back it was harder losing team-mates Sonny, Bernard and Lockers, than it was the coach.

Again things are soon forgotten, whether you are a player or coach, if you are winning. We enjoyed a tremendous winning run under McCrae which stretched through a total of 17 league and cup games.

He brought a lot to our camp, and a lot of influences picked up with being around the top players and coaches Down Under. He was also a pretty fair bloke and had that disciplined streak about him in that first year.

I also reckon he was grinning from ear to ear to have inherited a class side, with a good mixture of youth and experience. He knew he was on to a winner.

8

DOUBLE TOPS

It was easy to become disorientated because once the old centenary season finished, after barely a two-week break, the new term began for us with the Challenge Cup.

We had four straight cup rounds, going right up to the semi-final before the Super League had even started. It was hard to get your head round which season was starting and where it was ending.

Having said that, life was made a lot easier for me because I stopped working as a plasterer at the end of December 1995. I was the last player to go full-time at Saints because of my work. My full-time contract started on 1 January, 1996.

Shaun McCrae took over Saints' coaching reins in January and he brought on board some good ideas.

Getting to Wembley was our first objective of the season – and the disappointment of missing out on getting to the Cup Final in previous years really spurred us on in 1996.

This was a new coach, a new season and a new era and we began well, stringing some fantastic wins together. And we were getting to the finishing touches of nurturing everyone, with lads like Joey Hayes, Andy Haigh and Danny Arnold coming through the ranks.

We started the cup programme in blistering fashion away from home, putting 58 points on both Castleford and Rochdale in the opening two rounds of the Challenge Cup. Then while we were at Rochdale we were told of the biggest shock in the game for many a year. Salford had knocked Wigan out of the cup!

Wigan's fifth round exit at the Willows sent shockwaves through rugby league. In fact it was probably the biggest shock since the last time Wigan had been knocked out when Paddy Kirwan scored a late try for Oldham in 1987. Salford, who were not in Super League, just took their chances well and caught Wigan out.

It was kind of pleasing because Wigan had all the big game players and they had won the cup for eight years on the trot. Obviously it sends a buzz through the game when you realise the Challenge Cup is up for grabs and there is going to be new name on the trophy that year.

Nobody is invincible on a Challenge Cup afternoon and the Willows has never been a happy hunting ground as far as Wigan are concerned.

We played the winners in the following round and there was all kinds of talk that they were going to do the same to Saints. Some of our fans and officials reminded us that the Willows had been a graveyard for our cup hopes in the past. Alex Murphy had taken a highly fancied team there in 1988 and came off second best.

Well there was to be no repeat performance and we eased home 46–26 to book our semi-final spot. We got the draw we wanted, avoiding Leeds and Bradford to play first division Widnes at Central Park.

Although I had played at Wembley with both Great Britain and England, I was determined to get there with Saints.

The hurt and disappointment that you feel in losing a semi-final is one of the worst feelings in the game. It always sticks in your head – I was gutted when we lost to Leeds in the semi in 1994, and kept telling myself, 'We are not slipping up again'. To go so far in the cup and come away with nothing is tough. It is a hard, long day watching the Challenge Cup Final on television if you have fallen at that final hurdle – 80 minutes away from stepping out at Wembley. So we approached that game with caution, although it seemed to be a foregone conclusion that we were going to beat Widnes.

Widnes were a shadow of their former selves and had had to sell many of their star names and promising youngsters. In fact Saints had picked up a couple of players from Naughton Park. But they still had a couple of old heads in their ranks. This was a one-off game and I had been at Oldham when they had reached the semi-final in 1990. On that day Warrington were clear favourites, but the underdogs nearly pipped them. So I knew that the

Challenge Cup can be mad. Some Aussies can't understand the concept – even Ian Millward, when he first came to Saints, didn't fully grasp it and I bet he would admit that too. There are no second chances and who would have thought second division Salford could have beaten the mighty Wigan?

We did enough to win 24–14 to book our passage to Wembley and a meeting with Bradford. Unlike later years, we had a really long build-up to the final day – seven weeks in total. That lengthy period had its pros and cons. On the plus side it helped develop a bit of Wembley fever in the town, not that the fans needed much encouragement on that score. All the shops did Wembley window displays and there was a real buzz of excitement. Added to that there was no Wigan, and all the fans were saying, 'We have got a chance here!' They scented victory.

The extra time also allowed the club to get organised. Anybody who knows how Saints operate will understand that time was what they needed! They can take three weeks to post a letter, never mind order suits, book hotels and coaches. So away from the rugby side of things it was probably an advantage.

On the playing front it was a bit of a nightmare really. You are OK at first but as soon as it gets to two or one games before Wembley you start thinking, 'What if I get injured?' and that is the worst mental frame of mind to be in.

We played Halifax at Thrum Hall six days before Wembley. I can tell you that was never the easiest place to go to at the best of times. You always knew you were going to get a bit of a physical bashing going into a game ahead of a final. Your opponents know that if you are going to Wembley the following week the last thing you want is a battle. They sniff the chance of a shock and try to kick some ass and mix it, because they know you have Wembley on your mind.

The coach, more than anyone, is nervous, and Shaun McCrae probably thought to himself 'Six days before the final and I could lose my key players here!' That was a thinking that probably was not lost on Ian Millward some years later!

For players it strengthens you mentally if anything because you have to think, 'Hang on a minute, we have business to do first'.

And there was real business to do – we could not afford to drop points if we wanted to win that first ever Super League. In those first two seasons, before the concept of the Aussie-style Grand Final was hatched, the title went to the team finishing on top of the pile.

Super League kicked off in a blaze of glory – they launched the tournament in Paris, with the Aussie-packed French side taking on Sheffield in front of 18,000 fans.

This heralded the start of summer rugby and a bold new era. I know we don't live in the hottest climate in the world, but we are not used to heat in Britain. In fact we all moan if it is too hot. The majority of our games in that first season were played on Sunday afternoons at 3 o'clock and it was a case of 'Mad dogs and Englishmen go out in the midday sun!'

In many respects it suited Saints' style of play to be playing on firmer pitches instead of traipsing through mud. We had a fast team so it suited us down to the ground. Traditionally, Saints have always been a side that has preferred to play on the pitch rather than in it.

There were some very hot days in July and August particularly, but we were better educated in terms of playing requirements because we were now full-time professionals. We knew all about nutrition, diet and water intake. McCrae's experience of coaching players in a warmer climate Down Under also helped.

In terms of diet and nutrition, you learn more about it the more you progress. I class myself as a racing car – and you can't put four-star petrol in me, you have to put in eight star. Once I became a full-time professional, my diet was always bob on and that was boosted with the aid of supplements.

When I lived at home with my mum and dad – which I did until 2000 – it was very expensive for our family, particularly early on when it came to fuelling three rugby players.

My mum knew what the score was and we were always fed well. When I was working during the day all that grafting meant I could eat what I wanted because I knew I would burn it off. Once I finished work, I became more educated as a player about nutrition and started to look after myself a bit more.

You could see the pace of the game was increasing – all the

players were a lot fitter, and were training a lot harder. It was no longer a case of doing a shift down the pit or standing on scaffolding and then turning up to play a game. We were all becoming more athletic and those old school, less athletically built players, who didn't fit the bill only stuck around for a few years. The game was becoming faster and taking the defence ten metres back instead of five again worked in our favour. We all like to beat a man having time with the ball. That was another aspect that suited us, particularly with the strong players we had on our left hand side.

Our kick-off to the new summer era was a bit more modest than Paris – we trekked up to West Cumbria to play Workington Town. Going there in springtime is a damn sight better than going up there in the depths of winter. And the cash injection that the clubs had had meant that for the first time we could stop at a hotel on the way to Workington and have soup and sandwiches. Welcome to Super League!

But Workington could always be a tricky place to go and they had a lot to prove. However we needed a good start and got it with a 62–0 victory.

We followed that with a vital 41–26 win over Wigan on Good Friday, which once again underlined that perhaps the balance of power was tipping our way. The gap had been closing and I think in many ways Wigan had become victims of their own success.

Wigan had won the Middlesex Charity Sevens at Twickenham the previous May and then watched as players like Gary Connolly, Henry Paul and Inga Tuigamala went back to have stints in union. Wigan were the brand name in rugby and they received invitations because of that. After years of domination they must have found that season tough to take – particularly as it was Saints who seemed destined to take their crown. Our winning roll continued all the way up to Wembley.

We had come on by leaps and bounds, although we had won nothing yet. It was not like previous years when we were putting on big scores one week and losing the next. This year we were totally consistent in our play and performances.

The Challenge Cup Final was the last piece of the jigsaw. We had so many fans who had never seen Saints win the Challenge

Cup – it had been 20 years since the club had lifted the game's most famous trophy. You could see that everyone had been thinking about it and sensed that something was going to happen. In fact talk of 1976 was rammed down our throats so much that week.

The build-up was great and because Howesy was good at getting the money spent, we had a ball. We trained at Eton College and used their facilities for our finishing off sessions. Let's just say the Eton facilities were a touch different from my old school, St John Fisher.

One afternoon all the schoolboys were brought out to watch the training session and they appeared to be quite a timid bunch. One of the comedy moments there came with our big prop Adam Fogerty, who was with our squad even though he was getting a bit of work in the acting game. It was about that time that he had banjoed Jack Duckworth on Coronation Street. If you look at the size of Fog, he is a huge bloke with rugged features. Well half-way through the session at Eton, he was menacingly lurking on the touchline, all 6ft 5 of him, dripping with sweat. All the boys were fascinated by this big bruiser of a bloke until he turned round and growled 'What the bloody hell are you lot looking at!' You have never seen as many kids with fear in their eyes, they jumped out of their skins – even though he shouted 'I am only kidding' shortly afterwards.

The preparation was A1, with new suits and everything. Everybody was pretty nervous and although I had played in internationals at Wembley, this was my first Challenge Cup. I lost count of the number of times I was reminded that week of the game's many greats who have never played in a Challenge Cup Final. Here we were with a very young team and only Alan Hunte and Bobby Goulding had played in a Wembley Cup Final before.

When the team coach turned into Wembley Way there were thousands of fans all cheering us on, it was such an amazing feeling and a great sight to see. They stopped doing that with the coaches shortly afterwards, but at least we got that privilege in 1996. When we got to the end we came to those big gates of the tunnel where the outriders and team coaches drive in. I had watched so many teams do this on television, and here I was now doing it myself.

It was a scorching hot day and the crowd was really noisy and partisan. A Cup Final is a lot more personal than an international.

We were favourites that day, and rightly so after the performances we had been putting in prior to that game.

We had the game under control and were winning 12–8 thanks to two tries from Steve Prescott and one from Danny Arnold. I don't know what it was, whether it was because we had caned so many teams already that year, but we took our foot off the gas. Just before half time Bradford nudged ahead when Robbie Paul grabbed the first of his hat-trick of tries. They stretched that when our former team-mate Bernard Dwyer went over just after the break. I think we possibly got preoccupied with the heat – it was like playing in a furnace – but what we had to do was stop feeling sorry for ourselves and get back to playing.

At 26–12 down with 25 minutes remaining we were pretty close to falling apart I can tell you. We had a fair bit of lady luck on our side that day because to stop any side with such momentum you have to come up with something pretty special.

Then Bobbie Goulding put that first bomb up and as soon as their full-back Nathan Graham dropped it and Keiron Cunningham pounced on it we saw light at the end of the tunnel. That won us the game. It is a fact of life in the game, even today, that if a winger or a full-back drops one ball you do your best to get it up to them again as quick as you can while it is still fresh in their mind. That was what we did that day – it was bang, bang, bang. Simon Booth and Ian Pickavance grabbed similar scores from high ball spillages and that got us back in the game and then pushed our noses in front.

Bradford still came back at us and the game was still in the balance until Apollo Perelini smashed his way through for the clincher.

It was just great walking round the pitch afterwards carrying that cup. It was such a brilliant day – on a personal note I topped the tackle count on our side with 29, just ahead of Keiron and Apollo. There was a lot of leg tackling that day, which made the game even quicker. When you have the likes of Robbie Paul sidestepping on a sixpence you can't get much in the way of shoulder contact on them. You just grab at their legs, but that meant a quick play the ball and they were off again. It was so sapping energy wise.

I can't really remember much about the game because it went so quickly. Wembley tires the legs out – and you are shattered – but as soon as the final whistle goes you remember more about the celebrations than the game itself. You just know you have won and that is all that matters at Wembley.

We were at the after match 'do' and after a while a few of us, whose partners had not come down, decided we wanted a change of scenery so we set off for St Albans for the remainder of the night. Straight after the big function we jumped into taxis and headed out. For some reason we ended up going into Windsor, all suited and booted up for a big night out. When we got there we were so badly overdressed for the clubs that we stuck out like sore thumbs. After a night of people giving us funny looks, we decided we might as well get a cab back to the hotel but there were big queues in the taxi ranks.

There were a few of us, including Andy Northey, the club doctor, and my mate Ginger, weighing up our limited options when a bobby spotted us on the street and recognised us.

We told him we needed a taxi – and he told us to hang on a minute, he'd see what he could do. The next thing we see is this Black Maria and this sergeant told the driver to take all eight of us back to the hotel.

Before we left the hotel chairman Eric Ashton had told me that I was in charge and I was to make sure we did not get into trouble. So on the way back I looked at the doctor and one of the other lads sitting in the cage where they usually keep their police dogs and what Eric had said to me clicked. I thought this was too perfect a sketch to turn down. I leant over to one of the bobbies and asked if we could play a joke on our chairman. He was up for it but only if we gave him his helmet back, which one of our lads was wearing!

So we drove up to the front of the hotel, with lights flashing and I had to run in and get Eric out from the function room.

I told him, 'We are in a bit of trouble, the police have got some of our lads outside!' Well Ash is the most mild mannered of blokes, but he was not best pleased and got the club's solicitor, Howard Morris, to go and talk to the policemen outside.

As they walked out, it was like a scene from Rocky, where everyone followed in a line to be greeted by this Black Maria with the lights still flashing, glum players and a stony-faced cop.

Our solicitor asked, 'What seems to be the problem officer?'

But that was the cue for the van doors to swing open and for the lads to jump out and start rolling on the floor laughing! It took Eric about three months to see the funny side.

We headed back to St Helens the following morning and we had a civic reception at the Town Hall and the people came out in their thousands. They were hanging off lamp posts, standing on bush shelters, roofs, the window ledges, the statue of Queen Victoria, in fact every vantage point you can imagine in Victoria Square was occupied. It was an absolutely tremendous feeling – we had brought the cup back for the first time in two decades and the town was lapping it up.

I always preferred having the open top bus tour and reception on the Town Hall steps, to returning to the ground like they did in later years. It always felt that little bit more special.

Although we celebrated well, after winning the cup we were straight back into Super League action – and with the title going to the team finishing on top, we could not afford to drop any points. Every game that year was like a cup tie because we were the team to beat and everyone was raising their game against us. It was a combination of being cup holders and also being unbeaten in Super League and under McCrae. We were playing really intense games week in week out, which helped us at the business end of the season.

But because we had won a major trophy for the first time in 20 years it gave the players, and the town as a whole, a massive belief. Fans could also see that we were going to get better because of the young players we had brought through into the team.

We had a mental toughness that allowed us to win games by the odd point against the likes of London and Warrington. That inner strength probably stuck with us in the years that followed and that allowed us to win in often unlikely circumstances.

We also knew that if we didn't start very well that it was going to be a hard day at the office and that was always the case throughout my career.

During that run we played Sheffield in an 'on the road' fixture in Cardiff at the old Arms Park, which backs onto to the national stadium. It was a really hot day, but thankfully we had an evening kick-off. To keep ourselves occupied, Newy and myself ended up taking a guided tour around Cardiff Castle during the day. Everybody enjoyed that game – I have plenty of friends in Wales and they all made the effort to come and watch that match and they really lapped it up.

Because of the expansion of Sky coverage, rugby league was probably becoming more accessible to Welsh fans and out of a crowd of 6,000, around 4,000 were interested locals.

The Welsh had a hunger for rugby league – particularly as union was on a bit of a downer there at the time. It was a glorious opportunity for rugby league to push a new fresh product. They missed a chance then, but it seems as though a lot of amateur teams are now taking it up at conference level in places like Cardiff, Aberavon, Swansea and Bridgend, which can only be a good thing all round. I am sure there is enough money in Wales to start a franchise and there is no shortage of players.

Just look at the likes of Scott Gibbs, who made quite an impact at Saints. We were surprised when he returned to Wales in August that year after signing for Swansea. The barriers had come down allowing professionals to return to rugby union after previously being banned. He went on to do great things with the British Lions on their tour to South Africa.

Everybody was surprised that Gibbsy went back to union, but I had had previous conversations with him where he would say, 'This game is too hard for me'. He would also add that that he could earn the same money and maybe more playing union. He was glad he tried league and did a cracking job at it too.

Our winning run under Shaun McCrae predictably came to a halt at Central Park, losing to Wigan and then being beaten at Bradford a fortnight later. Once you lose two out of three in those circumstances some people start thinking the wheels have come off. But we had made a good start to the year and that is what saw us through.

It was a two-horse race at the top and with Wigan drawing their game with London, it meant all we had to do was keep on winning. We were in control of our own destiny – but it was a tough task. The key game in all this was our visit to the Valley to take on the Broncos. We all knew the game was vital, but London wanted to take the spoils. They had already taken a point off Wigan and I think they had something to prove against us.

Prior to the season starting there had been a lot of controversy over London's fast-track admission to Super League ahead of better placed northern teams like Keighley. They certainly meant business and wanted to establish themselves and rugby league in the capital.

We knew it was a pressure game and had the chance to be either heroes or nearly men.

I went over on my ankle and did my ligaments, so only played 23 minutes of that game. We knew it was going to be a toughie and it was. Apollo Perelini's try went down as the one that saved our bacon – and how vital it was too.

After leaving the field I had to watch the rest of the game from the portable buildings that were used as changing rooms in the corner of the Valley.

That London game's closeness has been repeated many times since – Saints never really trounce London and there are not usually many points in it. And you can guarantee that every time we have been to London since, be it to the Stoop, Brentford or the Valley, someone always says, 'It is going to be tough here. Do you remember when Apollo scored the try that won us the league?'

I missed a couple of games with my ankle injury – but every game from there on in was a must win one. That was followed up by running over to press 376 on Teletext to see how many Wigan had won by and how the league tables stood. Points difference had scuppered Saints' title hopes in 1993 and that is one of the main reasons I always checked out the for and against.

The destiny of the very first Super League title rested on the final game of the season and we had to beat Warrington. Former Saints' great Alex Murphy was their team manager at the time – and there was all this talk that he would have something up his sleeve for this one.

But we had come too far to slip up at the last hurdle particularly against a Warrington side that did not have the greatest of success rates at Knowsley Road.

It was a roasting hot August bank holiday weekend and the ground was absolutely packed with 18,000 people crammed in. The hairs really do stand up on the back of your neck when you have so many people inside a ground like Knowsley Road. They cheered our every move and try and we walked it. It was never in doubt.

Unfortunately I had to come off ten minutes from time after getting a crack from Vila Matautia. We both went in for the same tackle, but he caught me at the side of my eye and I came off worst needing five stitches. As a result I ended up missing the final whistle because I was being patched up on the sidelines. With stitches I am one of those players that says, 'Just get it over and done with'. The needle just goes straight in. If you are in the heat of the battle you just want to get out there again.

I was back on the pitch after the final whistle for the celebrations and the great parade at the end.

We could not have written a better script – to go so long without winning a major cup and then to win them both in the same year was a dream. With it being such a drought most fans would have been happy with just the Challenge Cup, but to win the pair of them was even better. You just get a taste for success and to win the first Super League trophy was a bit special. We had led the table from the front, which made it feel even better. In subsequent seasons, under a different format, we have won it from different places in the league, but that is the nature of the competition. We were the champions and it was a great feeling.

We could not complete the treble, losing 44–14 to Wigan in the Premiership Final at Old Trafford. I have the medal at home because I played in the semi, but I don't hold it in much regard because I didn't play in the game and therefore didn't deserve one.

Wigan were smarting a bit and probably had a bit to prove and we had already won enough. I missed the final because I was having my knee cleaned up in preparation for the tour to New Zealand.

That tour was initially scheduled to be an Ashes tour, but

because of the ARL/Super League war in Australia, it became a tour to Papua New Guinea, Fiji and New Zealand instead. I was gutted really because I had probably been one year too young to go on the previous Ashes trip back in 1992 and Great Britain never toured Australia again in the normal sense of the word. I feel as though I really missed out in that respect.

I was in the pomp of my career and had been looking forward to going on a proper Australia tour. This one they had thought up felt like a tin pot tour to me.

We kicked off in Papua New Guinea, and on our way there we stopped off in Singapore for about 12 hours. Phil Larder was coach and he was new to being the GB boss. He absolutely flogged us as soon as we got off the plane in Singapore. To make matters worse, on the way to that training session we saw a local bloke get knocked off his bike and killed. Our coach was right behind it when it happened and just drove around it. It was awful – about eight of the lads could not train after seeing that. I wish I had joined them.

Even though I could have done with another couple of weeks, I played in the Papua New Guinea Test match. It was the first and last time I had played in PNG and it was the most hostile environment I have encountered, conditions wise.

I am glad I went there mind, and sampled it for myself, but I would not want to go back. Papua New Guinea had just had their equivalent of a Challenge Cup Final and some of the supporters had been travelling for a week on foot to get to the game. When you get there and see what goes on it is hard to believe. There were gun cartridges on the pitch we had to train on. They had been fired to stop rival fans rioting at that previous day's cup final. We were meant to go and watch that game but had been delayed, which was probably a blessing in disguise. I picked the cartridges up and have kept them as a souvenir of my trip.

Our hotel was quite an ordeal too because it was not your standard Hilton. We had to cross a bridge from the reception area to our rooms over what was like part of a jungle. No matter how tough a rugby player we thought we were, when we were crossing that bridge at night with the sounds of wild animals howling all around us, we were faster than Carl Lewis doing the 200 metres.

We only just won that game against PNG, which was no surprise. It was a really tough match and I came off to get bandaged up after only ten minutes with blood streaming down my face after getting a PNG crack above the eye.

It was also unbelievably hot and in later years people would say to me, 'It is warm today, Joynty'. And I'd say, 'You want to go over and play in Papua New Guinea ...'

PNG had a few handy ploys that they used to their advantage too. When we were getting ready for that Test, they had all their pre-match tribal decorations and parades which meant we were lined up standing around waiting in the middle of the pitch in 100 degree heat. All their players were all stood in the shade muttering to each other, 'Look at these cranks here standing up in the direct sun'.

Whether it was a bit of my own keenness to impress, but it was the wrong decision to play in that game a week too soon. I went backwards from then and it ultimately cost me three weeks on tour.

Although I missed the Fiji game, I enjoyed going there because they put us up in this cracking hotel, which I think was used mostly by honeymooners. I was on rehab so spent most of the time in the finest hotel I have ever stayed in. I've always told Andrea that I would take her back there if I earned enough from playing, but I haven't yet!

By the time we got to New Zealand a lot of the lads were thinking about what the tour was all about. Were we proper Lions or was it a tin pot trip?

We were all confident of going to New Zealand and winning the series, but it just didn't happen.

Morale was not helped when we heard that players were being sent home as part of a cost-cutting exercise. When you go on tour you end up having a Test team and midweek team. Well the authorities said they were running out of money and so a lot of the lads from the midweek team were told to pack their bags and return to England. That should not have happened, particularly as we had been staying in the plushest hotels all tour. The irony was that at the time we were told we were staying in one of the best hotels in Auckland. It just did not add up.

The lads who remained on tour would have been happy to stay in less luxurious digs to allow everybody else to stay on because as soon those lads left it had a massive impact on the Test team morale. You build up friendships on tour and all of a sudden your mates are not there. Team Manager Phil Lowe did a cracking job, but maybe he just did not get the RFL's backing.

That demoralisation shows in the pattern of the results. We lost the First Test by five points, the Second by three and the last one 32–12. That was probably the biggest indication of plummeting team morale.

We played the Second Test at Palmerston North and you would not send your worst enemy there. There is nothing going on there, it is like a ghost town.

The Kiwis had a big prop called Grant Young and in the First Test he came out of the line to smash me, but I just kicked off my left foot so he didn't crack me as hard as he could have. He still knocked me off balance. It looked spectacular and they used that clip on television adverts which read, 'Come and see the Kiwis smash the Poms!'

After that series I was just glad to get back on the plane and think to myself 'Thank goodness for the rest', even though I knew it was only going to be a short one. I had played back-to-back rugby since the start of August 1994.

Some of the Saints lads got even less of a rest and had to play Wigan on Boxing Day and in the first week of the New Year in the Norweb Challenge. Sixteen thousand people turned up for the first one and 10,000 for the one at Saints. It was just a money-making ploy to get the turnstiles ticking over, but it was not fair to the fans or the players. The players were playing out of season and the fans got poor entertainment as a result.

It was just a ludicrous idea, but it was probably at about that time when clubs were wondering what they had done with all their money. They must have thought, 'We need to get another game on to get some cash!' I was glad to be sitting those games out.

9

CAPTAINCY CALLS

There is an old adage in this game, 'If you are going to win anything, you have to beat the best'. That is exactly what we thought to ourselves when our name came out of the hat, followed immediately by Wigan's for the opening round of the 1997 Challenge Cup. I have carried that thought throughout my playing career, but was really pleased that it was a home tie nonetheless.

Wigan were obviously still smarting from the previous year, after being dethroned as the game's cup kings. They had had it all their own way for so long and for Saints to be the club that took the double off them must have been even more galling for them and their fans.

The fact that I was born, brought up and still lived in Wigan meant I had a grin like a Cheshire Cat after that 1996 season. But I knew, more than most, that you soon get that smile knocked off your face when you come to another season because you have to do it all again. You are only as good as your next game.

That tie was a big occasion on three fronts: we were defending our cup, it was against our oldest rivals and because we were being beamed out live to four million viewers on BBC *Grandstand*, which was a lot more than watched rugby league on Sky.

The match could have been a disaster though, because our skipper Bobbie Goulding went high on Wigan prop Neil Cowie and in a split second he was red carded and off down the tunnel. We knew we were going to be up against it with only 12 men on the park, but what was fabulous about that day was everybody stuck to their guns.

Wigan never really had so much as a sniff that day. It was 10–10 at half time but we had real belief that afternoon. I don't like using 'belief' because you only use words like that on special occasions, but that match was one of those.

There was a really raucous crowd there, particularly up on the Popular Side, and the fans knew it was a real backs-to-the-wall effort from all of our lads. All the neutrals watching at home were backing the underdogs too, because we were a man down.

That was the first time really that I skippered the team and as vice-captain I stepped into the breach – I lapped it up. This was effectively the start of me becoming the club skipper and I really enjoyed the extra pressure. All of a sudden you are not just looking after your own game, you are responsible for taking care of the team. To beat Wigan with 12 men was a tremendous start, so it is one of those jobs that you could say I eased into.

What made me laugh was, after beating Wigan, everybody said, 'Well, you have to get to Wembley now!' Still, we got there comfortably, beating Hull, Keighley and Salford on the way. The cup run got us off to a great start to the year and that is all any sportsman wants.

Rugby league was experiencing one of its clampdowns on high tackles, and as such we lost Goulding, our captain and kicker, through a six-match suspension which was tough on the team. But every cloud has a silver lining and our bonus came in fetching in young Lee Briers – a teenager who only lived a drop kick away from the ground.

He was Saints mad and we used to call him Casper after the young lad who kept the hawk in the film *Kes*. Lee played outstandingly well and in those six games, although slight in frame and supposedly vulnerable in defence, he tackled everything that was thrown at him. It just doesn't sink in for lads when they are thrown in quickly like that; they just roll their sleeves up and get on with it.

We eased past Salford in the semi-final at Central Park, winning by 50 points to 20. It was a close game early on but I scored just before the break and remember former Wigan and Great Britain prop Andy Platt sliding off me as I went over the line and thought, 'This is a dream come true this one!'

One of the hardest parts of the afternoon was being interviewed by the BBC after the final hooter. In one short interview I broke the record for the most 'You knows' in three minutes! I had said all I wanted to say, but I could see the bloke at the side of me winding his hands around saying, 'Keep going'. Our match had probably finished a couple of minutes before they had anticipated and the Beeb had an extra couple of minutes to fill before the soccer teleprinter came on. I remember years later going to a dinner and somebody had dug the video out and presented it to me.

We were playing so well, and we knew that again we were the team to beat. We only lost one game ahead of the cup final, losing 13–12 to Leeds. They had raised their game and they did us although Goulding scored near the posts in the last minute, his conversion hit the post and bounced out. We were all gutted in the dressing room afterwards because that ended our winning run.

Even though we were playing well, Saints were still after strengthening the team and at this stage the 'Iestyn Harris saga' was dragging on. There was this talk of 'will he, won't he' join us from Warrington which generated a lot of hot air. Negotiations were quite serious, but it had no impact on our team because we had a more than capable stand-off half in Tommy Martyn. If the team needed strengthening, it was a case of needing another couple of forwards, not another half-back. The issue was not really a topic of conversation in the dressing room. It was a case of, 'Well, let's see if he turns up first and then we will start thinking about it'.

I am sure all the talk of bringing in a player like Harris, who at that time was one of the game's young stars, did spur Tommy on because he started that season outstandingly. At that time it was all about starting games and getting picked in the 13, so there would have been no question of either of them being content to sit on the bench.

There was some movement between the clubs – unfortunately it was in the other direction from Saints to the Wires and I was very sad to see Lee Briers leave. In particular, I was very disappointed to see him miss out on going to Wembley that year when he was sold to Warrington a few weeks before the final.

I know Bobbie Goulding was something of a folk hero in St Helens at that stage, but in Briers, Saints were letting go of one of their prize young assets. I don't know the ins and outs of the cash situation, but I knew that this lad had a lot to offer. He was a local kid who had done all his kicking about with the rest of those young lads, just a stone's throw away from the ground. He was exactly the sort of lad who you wanted playing for Saints – he was begging for a contract.

Just before Lee departed, we went to Paris and we took him as the travelling reserve. I think his main job on that trip was to collect 20 francs off everybody, and then trot off to the supermarket to get the ale in for us all.

The funny thing about the Paris game was that the club tried to get as many fans over as possible, not only to boost support, but to also cut the overall costs. As a result players would end up rooming next door to fans, which was quite an unusual situation. So we would be trying to get a bit of a rest before the big game and there would be somebody knocking on your door asking you about the game, who was playing or where there was a nice restaurant. The fans were great and they turned up in droves and really enjoyed the trip, but when you are trying to get your head round playing a Super League match it is not the best preparation.

Still we won out there and the players all had a good drink afterwards and there were quite a few sore heads on the plane. It was something different to the south of France, which was more traditional rugby league territory. A change is as good as a rest, they say, but the next new venue was a bit trickier.

The week before the Challenge Cup Final we played our home game against Castleford at Anfield. It was a game we could have done without to be honest, the week before a big final, but we had to play although I would have preferred playing in more familiar surroundings.

It felt really odd running out at one of the most famous sports grounds in the world in front of 12,000 fans, with three almost completely empty sides. Only the Kop was full, with a couple of hundred people scattered in the main stand. The memories I have of Liverpool as a footie fan was seeing 44,000 people packed in there, swaying and singing, so it did feel a bit of a strange experience.

Playing that game there was a massive risk for the club at that time of the year because we were at Wembley the following week. That was all the lads were thinking about, not the experience of playing on Anfield's famous turf. It would have been nice to have played there later on in the season to fully appreciate it without just thinking, 'I hope I don't get injured here and miss Wembley next week'. That took a bit of the shine off it.

We came through unscathed – and then it was all eyes on Wembley. Our super efficient chief executive David Howes could organise a good trip. From getting measured up for our suits to running out on the pitch, he had made sure Wembley '97 ran like clockwork.

The day before the game we were relaxing at a summer house owned by Eton College, playing electronic clay pigeon shooting, with the barbecue on, pool tables going and watching young Andy Northey causing chaos in the middle of the Thames by clowning around on a rowing boat. It was good laugh, but any outsiders looking in were probably thinking, 'These men have got a big game tomorrow? No way!'

But it was a fantastic operation, with everything catered for. The only thing that looked as though it had thrown a spanner in the works was the bomb scare on the morning of the match, and Wembley had to be evacuated while it was checked over.

It was bad timing really because we had just boarded the coach and had just left the hotel when the police motorcycle outriders, who escort the bus all the way to Wembley, received a call that there was a bomb scare. They held the bus up and nobody knew whether it was going to be a matter of minutes or a couple of hours. All the lads were sat there on a stationary bus in the baking heat with a suit and stiff collar on, which was not much fun. Everybody was getting tetchy and agitated, but nobody could go anywhere. It was pretty stressful – everyone just wanted to get there.

Despite that little hiccup, the build-up and preparation for the final was even better than the previous year. There were not many newcomers among our ranks so the majority of that 1997 team had played in the previous year's epic triumph. Because of that our camp was a lot more at ease and that gave us an edge. The reverse was probably the case for Bradford, so all of a sudden they were under pressure instead of us, the favourites.

Bradford were the club that had embraced the American-style

Super Bowl razzamatazz more than most since the switch to summer. They were probably the trendsetters as a club off the field, transforming their image from dull and dour old 'Northern'. They did plenty of talking about how they had trebled their crowds since the switch to summer, but could not come up with the goods when it came down to it on the park against the Saints.

The form book goes out of the window when it comes to the big matches, it all comes down to who wants it more. Because we had had a taste of success, we did not want to be coming back from Wembley with losers' medals. There was that massive desire to win and then we could think about having a good night.

As for the game itself, I thought our forwards laid a very good platform and that allowed the individual skills of the players to shine that day. Although Bradford fielded quite a big, experienced pack with Brian McDermott, Sonny Nickle, Bernard Dwyer, Paul Medley and Steve McNamara, I thought our forwards got the upper hand up front.

It was a really energy sapping encounter though. I played in my usual left-sided back row slot, but ten minutes before half time everybody was dead on their feet and I had to take a drive up the right hand side because we had nobody there to take it in. That is how shattered everyone was and half time could not have come soon enough.

But we came out and kept at it in the second half, and the rest is history as they say. The icing on the cake for me was scoring a try, which was a great feeling. I had scored at Wembley before with England, but this was an even better feeling.

There were gaping holes appearing in Bradford's defence and I actually tipped Tommy Martyn off at the previous tackle. I said, 'Tommy, just drop me off here, I can drive a bus through that!'

And as we had done about 120 times in the past, and a thousand times in training, he dropped me off 20 metres out and it was like the parting of the waves. There was a bit of a race to the line because their Great Britain full-back Stuart Spruce was hurtling across, but I had already done him really. It was a crucial try as well in the game, there was no way they were coming back at us.

I went up to pick up the Challenge Cup for the first time – with new deputy Prime Minister John Prescott presenting it. Labour had won the general election two days before the final.

The decision that I would go up to lift the trophy instead of Bobbie Goulding had already been arranged because I had led the team through all the other cup rounds. I always knew that as soon as we won that Cup, I was going up the steps to collect it, which was an added incentive for me to play well that day.

Although I did not toss the coin in the middle, I captained the team on the day of the final. Picking up the trophy was not a spur of the moment gesture from Goulding – he had already been told that this was happening, although it may not have looked like that from the stands and on the television.

Looking back on that Challenge Cup win you see the names of quite a few young lads in there like prop Andy Leathem and centre Andy Haigh. For quite a few years since then it has been a case of, 'Where are they now?' But at least they can look back at their Challenge Cup winner's medals. Those lads took their chances well then and got their just rewards. Having said that, I am surprised Andy Leathem did not go on to do better things, although he did suffer from an illness.

Following the game we went into that big bar at Wembley, which can only be described like going into a big long church hall. There were no proper seats; it's just a free for all with the likes of Parky, Bernard Cribbins and Colin Welland in there. You get all the players' families gathered in there star spotting.

As we got stuck into our post match celebrations, David Howes told me that he had to go back up to Saints to sort the homecoming celebrations out. So he put me in charge and said, 'Tell the lads that the free bar is shutting in 15 minutes'. Everyone was having such a great time though, so I told him that he would either have to tell them himself or give me his room number to charge the account to.

He said, 'I can't tell them I am too busy'. But I was adamant, so he ended up giving us his room number. There were probably about 30 of us left when the free bar shut, but I came up with the magic number of Howesy's room.

The homecoming itself, which was staged at Knowsley Road, was not as good as the previous year. You can't beat having it on the

Town Hall steps with people packed into the square. Everyone was confined to one space at Saints, so the bus trip round town was not as good because they had all gone up to the ground.

For the lads, one of the best parts of winning at Wembley is the trip home, especially when the bus is well loaded up with drink. None of us had had any sleep the night before, so if you top up what you have had the night before with another three pints, you are on your way to getting well oiled again. We stopped off at an off-licence just outside of London and cleaned the place of everything. I think the owner must have thought Christmas had come early. Anyway two hours from the ground we had run out of beer on the top deck, but chairman Eric Ashton put a stop to us getting any more from the boot, saying, 'There is no way you lads are going up on stage in front of 10,000 people in this condition!' So we had a two-hour sobering up period, which was perhaps as well. People ask you afterwards about what gibberish you muttered on the mike at homecomings. Half of the players could not even tell you who had interviewed them never mind what they had said. It is a crazy idea really getting on a platform, but you can't beat parading the cup to the fans. Maybe we should just have walk-on silent parts!

I was quite happy with things at the club and the way we were going. In Mike Gregory, who was Shaun's assistant coach at the time, we had a person who I had always looked up to as a player. He went to the same school as me and had grown up in Wigan, played for St Pat's like me and scored that famous full-length try for Britain in that third test against the Aussies in 1988. Mike was probably only on the first rung of the coaching ladder and the game was, understandably, probably a little bit in front of him. He was not yet the coach he was later to become at Wigan.

That is purely a time thing – but you have to start somewhere and it is one thing I will bear in mind should I want to start coaching. Becoming a coach is far different than playing; Greg probably found it more difficult because he had only just finished playing. But it put him in good stead. He was defence mad, mind. All he used to talk about was marker defence.

There was a long hard season ahead of us after the Wembley win. Once the champagne bubbles had drifted off, reality hit home straight away. As fate would have it, the fixture planners had kindly put us down for a trip to Odsal the following week.

We were duly hammered by the revenge-seeking Bulls and I was stuck on the bench, playing only the last 10 minutes or so. Everyone at Saints was content with winning the Challenge Cup, but maybe we started taking things for granted. We went through a shocking spell drawing with London, losing to Salford and getting stuffed 65–12 by Wigan at home. We had hit the slide big time.

Without naming names, some people had got too big for their boots and had become a law unto themselves. It badly needed the organisation to set some guidelines on discipline. It was not coming from the players and the coach at the time could only do so much. It needed to come from the top, but it never did. Sometimes it is much easier to clown around rather than be disciplined and focused, but that does not win you matches.

It was at this point that I had to go to the club and voice my concerns. I knew standards were slipping and I told the board something that went along the lines of, 'You either sort this out or we will lose the plot completely here and go under'.

That was the only demand I made on the club – I wanted us to be put back on track. I was not after more money or another contract, it was a purely a case of telling them that the ship needed steadying. I told director Mally Kay to either sort it out or I would be on my way to another club.

Mally Kay had anticipated my concerns over what was going on, and came to me to hear my views. He had tremendous man-management skills and was blunt. He is not the sort of bloke who minces his words, which is a quality I like in people. Mally would make a good manager because he had the skills on how to motivate adults on a day-to-day basis. He knew which ones needed a rollicking and those who needed an arm round their shoulder. Mally also had a knack of ringing up when you needed him to.

With things going badly, probably the last thing we could have done with was the visit of three top Aussie sides in the World Club Championship.

The concept for the new international club tournament

probably did not do the British game any good at all, if anything it was a complete waste of money. That cash could have been pumped into a lot better places than this mismatched, badly thought out competition. I could see what they were aiming for as a concept, but it was just the wrong time all round.

Every club probably had not really got over the shock of the impact of Super League and were getting the accountants out to look at their books to see what they were all spending.

Saints were drawn in a group which included Auckland Warriors, Penrith Panthers and Cronulla Sharks, and we played them home and away. We didn't do ourselves any justice at home – we were tonked in all three games but we did perform better on our travels.

Looking back I think we were just looking forward to going to play Down Under. It was a case of, 'Let's get the home games out of the way and get to Oz and New Zealand!' That was the way most of the lads were thinking.

I was a bit concerned, however, when I rolled up at the club for a 7am departure to Australia to be greeted by the sight of about five of our lads with their hair dyed blond. I was thinking, 'All we need now is the buckets and spades and the Union Jack shorts!' It was not about that – and we had a couple of lads who were in holiday mode, although I am not singling those 'blond' lads out particularly.

Newy, who lives in Yorkshire, got stuck on the motorway and so he missed our coach to the airport. He rang Mally Kay up and told him the situation, but the players knew nothing about it. There were always plenty of tales knocking about that Newy didn't like flying, which was a load of rubbish.

Anyway, we got to Amsterdam after flying from Manchester via Heathrow, and there was an announcement saying, 'Can Chris Joynt make himself known to the cabin crew?' Well, with it being Amsterdam and its reputation you begin to think of all kinds of things. I kept thinking somebody had planted drugs in my bag or something daft like that. The cabin crew had said that directors Eric Ashton and Howard Morris, who were travelling business class as opposed to the players, who were in cattle class, needed to speak to me. I found them and they told me that Newy was at

Heathrow and they wanted me to fly back and meet him and bring him over. I weighed it up and thought about all the waiting around I would have to do and said, 'No way!'

They ended up calling in young Jason Johnson, who was working at the ground at the time as a Super League Trainee, and he ended up accompanying Newy. They probably knew Newy couldn't do tasks like checking in, so they got a 17-year-old kid to chaperone him all the way to Australia.

We gave a good account of ourselves once we got over there and had a good trip. I know Auckland thrashed us, but we competed well with Cronulla and Penrith.

Auckland had former Saint Tea Ropati in their ranks and he did a fair bit of damage against us. The Warriors also had Matthew Ridge at full-back and young Stacey Jones at scrum half and were a formidable side.

We had two minibuses taking us to training and saw massive advertising hoardings before the Cronulla game which said, 'See the Poms used as Shark bait!' It didn't make us nervous, just gave us something to laugh at.

The other good thing about that trip was that the entire squad went on it. The Super League paid for the first 21 players, and we raised the money ourselves for the other squad players to go. The lads got one signed shirt each to raffle off for £100. If they didn't want to sell raffle tickets they threw in the money instead and that way every one got to go.

Although we lost all our games, they had concocted a system that ensured some European teams undeservedly qualified into the knockout stages of the competition and we beat Paris St Germain for the privilege of playing Brisbane Broncos in the next stage. Having lost all six of our group games, it showed we didn't deserve to be in the quarter-final because we got butchered by Brisbane.

Broncos used to have a mascot on horseback that ran round the pitch every time they scored. After we went 10 points down early on, we were stood behind the posts and Newy said, 'I hope they have another horse on standby because that one is going to be knackered before full-time!' Talk about gallows humour!

I had been made captain in August and prior to that the way

certain things were going I knew it was going to happen. I am not saying I was the ideal candidate for the job, but I was already vice-captain. I'm sure there were other names in the hat, but what probably stood me in good stead was taking the side to Wembley. Keiron Cunningham was pretty established by then, but perhaps he was considered too young.

You learn more as you do the job. The toss-up and which way to play is the captain's call, but everyone has an opinion. I tended to ask the kickers to take into account the wind or I would ask full-back Paul Atcheson or Wello if they had judged the sun. If I was a captain playing at Featherstone, with a notoriously big slope, I would always choose to play uphill first half and let them chuck everything at us then it would be easier in the second half.

Actually in the game, you learn a few tricks as you go along and how you play the referee can be the difference between winning and losing.

The likes of both the Connollys, Russell Smith and Karl Kirkpatrick were always sound with me. These blokes are part time refs and it is only the dedication of the men in the middle that makes sure they can keep up with the pace of the game. They should make refereeing full-time too if they want to get the quality up further.

I was never sent off in my career, but have been sin-binned twice for lying on. Perhaps one of the rule changes they should consider should be letting you lie on more if you are over 30! There is an art to it and it is vital to slowing your opponents' play the ball down.

The key to lying on without getting penalised is to keep moving, and if you are really good at it, turn and look to the referee as you are doing it. As long as the ref can see you are moving, you will get away with it.

If you simply lie on top of your opponent like a dead fish you will get penalised. In a match, if I could lie on I would do it and you could test refs out.

Karl Kirkpatrick, for example, would generally not be bothered about me lying on; he was always far too busy getting my team-mates back 25 metres! I used to love it when Karl reffed, and some days I thought about packing my quilt and a pair of pyjamas in my kit back once I knew he was in charge.

Bradford romped away with the Super League title that year, but we finished with a bit of a flourish, winning our last five league games. We got through to the final of the Premiership, which was still under the old top eight knockout system. It was the last time they had it as a Premiership, before the Grand Final system was introduced. Although it was another big day at Old Trafford for us, it just did not happen on the day against Eric Hughes' Wigan side.

There was still no end in sight for some of us and the GB lads had a Test series against Australia's Super League team in November. Rugby League was split down the middle in Australia due to the ARL/Super League conflict and as a result they brought a team made up only of players signed up to Super League clubs.

In some ways Great Britain, coached by former Wigan forward Andy Goodway, was on a hiding to nothing. Had we won that series people would have rattled off all the players who the Aussies could not select and claim it as a hollow win. Once again we were told that this was the best chance we ever had of winning a series.

They still brought some outstanding players and they had a few points to prove and they were also under some pressure back home. For a start they had outstanding ball handling prop Darren Britt, who later signed for Saints. And the Smith brothers, Jason and Darren, played exceptionally well that series.

They were like proper test matches, even though the Aussies could not wear the traditional Kangaroo green and gold strip.

It was good to return to Wembley again, because we had always started the series well in previous openers at Wembley. Reality kicked in when we lost that First Test, but we stuck in there and were determined to make amends.

That Second Test at Old Trafford really made the hairs stand up on the back of my neck. To walk out in front of a crowd as noisy as that, to strains of 'Land of Hope and Glory' was amazing.

It was also do-or-die for GB because we were used to going into the third test, with the series still alive at one-all. I was partnering Leeds' Adrian Morley in the second row that day and remember having a good game. We got the win we needed – a tremendous one at that and just recall running across and big Gordon Tallis taking me out. As I looked up Andy Farrell was going through to score. That win kept the series alive.

The final test at Elland Road, Leeds, proved to be a bit of a let-down – the Aussies played very well and won 37–20. That defeat marked the end of a very long year and to be perfectly honest, I was probably looking forward to a rest by that stage. We played a lot of rugby that year, with a lot of travelling thrown in as well.

10

GOING BACKWARDS

There had been a few comings and goings at the club, but our style of play stayed more or less the same. Saints had spent heavily on recruiting the highly rated loose forward Paul Sculthorpe from Warrington, for a record transfer fee for a forward – £300,000 plus Chris Morley. From our previous season's cup winning line-up Alan Hunte, Simon Booth and Steve Prescott all went to Hull, who had won promotion to Super League after the departure of Paris and my former club Oldham. Saints also brought in a couple of Aussies, big prop Brett Goldspink from Oldham, and centre Damien Smith.

Scully had been the kingpin of the Warrington side and he was a good capture for us. It was a bit of a downside for him, especially because the price tag around his neck weighed him down at times and he did not immediately live up to people's expectations because he was not performing instant miracles.

At Warrington Scully was their main man who did almost everything, but here Saints had players who could play a bit of football too. He simply had to slot into the second row and adjust to his new job. It took him a while to find his feet, but professional sport is cruel and people want instant success. He had quite a few critics early on that year.

Scrum half Sean Long, who had joined towards the back end of the previous year, established himself in the side, although Bobbie Goulding was still at the club. Longy had sneaked in from First Division Widnes, after starting his career off at his home town Wigan.

He must have suffered a few knocks at Wigan but in hindsight they must have kicked themselves for letting him go to Widnes in exchange for Lee Hansen. Longy gradually built himself back up at Naughton Park, so when you talk about being at the right place at the right time the timing was superb for Longy to come into our team.

We needed a good start to 1998 but not much had changed in the coaching of the team. We were stagnant in many respects, and ideas-wise we had not moved on from 1996. The players were keen and willing to learn, but coach Shaun McCrae's ideas were running out. The other teams had learned and cottoned on to our style of play, so it was always going to be tough battling three years on the trot with the same tactics.

We started that year reasonably well, but kept losing to the big teams – Bradford, Leeds and Wigan. All the time McCrae was at Saints we never won at Odsal and we very rarely beat Wigan.

Maybe it was a case of McCrae tending to concentrate more on the opposition ahead of a game, rather than us as a team. Sometimes we would walk out after a team meeting thinking, 'Bloody hell! This Wigan team are going to take some beating on Friday!' because they had been put up on such a pedestal.

What Shaun was trying to do in meetings like that was to protect himself by telling you, 'Make sure Farrell doesn't do you with a left foot step' or 'Watch Radlinski supporting on the inside!' so when it happened he could say afterwards he told you so. You can imagine playing a side like Wigan, they would have 13 players who could do it. In most games against Wigan, my job has been to police Farrell and I reckon I have probably done a good job on balance.

But with our lads looking out for all Wigan's attributes meant that it gave us less time to concentrate on our own game. We went into many of those games with the opposition built up too much from early on in the week and in some cases we were beaten before kick-off.

After beating Featherstone and Warrington in the early rounds, we said goodbye to the Challenge Cup we had held for the past two seasons after getting knocked out by Wigan in the quarter-final at Central Park. Wigan had moved on, and so had Leeds and Bradford.

Our new prop Goldspink had a good season and attracted the

interest of other clubs, namely Wigan. He ended up signing for them about three months before the season ended and although he probably got a bit of flak from the terraces, it was very rarely discussed among the players. There would be the odd wisecrack before a game like 'You are up against your own team today Brett!'

It is not a situation I would have enjoyed. When you sign a contract you must honour it, but with the cut-throat world of rugby league there is always something going on and lads need to sort out their futures.

That season we took another on the road game to Wales, playing Wigan at Swansea's Vetch Field. We had already lost to them three times that year and we lost this one 36–2. It turned out to be a bad day all round when events later in the evening left a sour taste and things were said that should not have been which resulted in Goulding being forced to leave the club. Read into that what you want!

It was not all gloom and doom that year, there were pluses – particularly the start of young Paul Wellens' career. He was like a scrawny little lad then, but what a player he has turned into. You could just see there was so much he wanted to learn and he just oozes St Helens rugby league.

He used to talk non-stop – 'Do you remember when you scored that try against Wigan?'

He would recall all the games he watched as a ten-year-old speccy and talk as if I was 50 years older than him. The transition from him being an ordinary lad off the terraces to getting a place on the bench happened so quickly for him. I think you get the best out of lads like that – it was the same with Lee Briers, Andy Northey, Lockers, Bernard Dwyer and Paul Forber. Local lads will give their heart and soul to the club. There is talk that local players at Saints have a history of being badly treated contract-wise, with the idea that they should be expected to play for local pride. But Wello is switched on enough to realise that rugby league is his business now and he is more than a Saints fan. He handles both sides really well and he still has time for fans because he remembers being in the stands not that long ago.

It was not just the big teams, Wigan, Leeds and Bradford, who we lost to that year. Once again we struggled against Sheffield

Eagles. We had a bad record at the Don Valley Stadium – I think it was because usually there were more people around our house for Sunday dinner than in there. The entire crowd was stacked on one side of the bowl and there was nobody in 80 per cent of the stadium. It was like playing on a patch of grass in the middle of nowhere, with just no atmosphere because the running track around the pitch meant the fans were miles away. And with every Tom, Dick and Harry knocking about in the corridors, it was just like playing at a council-run sports centre. We always struggled at Sheffield – it was one of those things. At least we had a good reason to lose to them that year because that was the year the Eagles beat Wigan in the biggest shock in Wembley history.

Saints were well off the pace that season, losing eight league games, finishing fourth behind Wigan, Leeds and Halifax. We finished seven points behind Halifax, and an incredible 13 behind the league leaders, Wigan.

Under the new play-off system, we still had a hope of becoming the champions even though we finished fourth! A lot of people did not understand the system at first, because it was different to the old sudden death top eight Premiership. The higher up you finish, the better chance you have of winning it, which became obvious that autumn.

The top three had two bites if they lost a game that year, but for us, it was sudden death. We beat Bradford at home before accounting for Halifax away in the semi-final eliminator. It was surprising to see how well Halifax had done that season with former Leigh and Wigan loose forward John Pendlebury in charge, but credit to them.

Our reward was a visit to Headingley the following weekend, but it was a game too far and our Super League dream was over. Wigan ended up winning the first ever Grand Final, beating Leeds at Old Trafford thanks to a Jason Robinson try.

At Saints it seemed everybody knew Shaun McCrae's contract was not going to be renewed. It was a surprise to some because he had brought so much success and the club was out of the doldrums. Shaun had fantastic attributes, but because other teams were getting better we needed something else. His man management skills were excellent as were some of his coaching techniques. If I ever go into coaching, I will certainly take a lot of those things with me.

What the players needed that year was a bigger challenge from the coaching side of things and some new ideas for the following season.

But what we were lacking more than anything was discipline and the players had gone into Champagne Charlie mode. The club was off the rails in more ways than one. As well as swapping players, the club at management level was changing and David Howes had also left.

The season did not finish there because once again we had an international series, this time against the Kiwis. They had whitewashed us on our ill-fated tour there in 1996 and there were hopes that we could turn things around.

We lost the First Test 22–16 at Huddersfield and their try just before the break proved crucial. It was a controversial incident because the hooter sounded as one of the Kiwis was tackled. We made the cardinal error of turning away, as if to head for the tunnel, but the ref let them play the ball and from close range big Joe Vagana bustled his way over for a try. Newy still ribs me about it today – but then again he doesn't watch much rugby!

I was in the frame when it happened, but I think everyone was anticipating half time. These are the things in the game that you learn from. Maybe the refereeing decision was not the best, but there you go. Late in the game Robbie Paul tackled Keith Senior in mid-air when all he had to do was catch it and score. Some argued that should have been a penalty try, with the kick under the sticks to level it, rather than just the penalty that we were awarded. Still sometimes decisions don't go your way.

There were no excuses for the Second Test, where we got murdered at Bolton's Reebok Stadium in front of over 28,000 fans. We led 16–8 at half time but they rattled in 28 unanswered points in the second half.

I started in the second row, but was subbed after 21 minutes and then brought back on 11 minutes into the second half. I was back on the bench again seven minutes from time. It was quite a frustrating series.

Andy Goodway was still the GB coach and there seemed to be

a big Wigan influence in his selection policy and he seemed to talk mostly to his Wigan stars. Everybody else was left on the sidelines and I used to think, 'If this is international rugby then I don't really want to be a part of it – I want a new challenge'.

Although I had plenty of respect for Goodway as a player, at that time I honestly believe his coaching methods didn't work with the Great Britain team. He had ideas that he could not quite get over to the players, and because they did not understand it he used to get so wound up that the training sessions used to end up in chaos. His frustration used to be left on the training field. He would end up shouting and would more or less walk off muttering, 'You thick bastards!' Probably what was needed was a more simplified game plan, because half of the players were worried about doing the wrong thing.

It is bad enough being an international coach at the best of times, given the limited amount of time you have with the players – but all of a sudden he was trying to bring in new ideas and concepts of how the team should play. It was just too much in too short a space of time. That proved his downfall in the end. If he coached in today's game he would probably be successful. Goodway was probably too advanced for his time as the Great Britain coach.

With the series lost we went to Watford's Vicarage Road ground for the Third Test aiming to stop a whitewash. Now Watford was no Wembley – and I am not sure if there was something wrong with their floodlights, but it seemed as though 20 bulbs had gone out on each pylon. There was dullness about the place but it seems to get a few big games. I don't know what the attraction was. It was like playing it in a Subbuteo stadium. It was not a ground that inspired us, so I could not understand taking important games like that 'on the road'. You want every advantage possible when you play the Kiwis or the Aussies because when we go over there they give us nothing.

We ended up drawing that game because Tony Smith grabbed a late drop goal. Personally I don't think draws count if you have lost the first two tests on your home soil – it was not classed as a whitewash, but in my eyes it was.

Playing at night in Watford was so forgettable I have trouble remembering anything about that game. Going home I kept thinking 'Is this what it's all about, playing rugby league 11 months of the year, ending up playing a prestige game on a gloomy soccer ground in Watford?'

At that stage I had lost my early enthusiasm for international rugby. You used to think about all the epic tours and test series, but this was different. There were none of the things that spurred me on to play for Great Britain. Maybe it was because these games were always at the end of such long seasons and everybody was in need of a break. All of a sudden using those autumn months to take a rest seemed an appealing option.

11

A YEAR WITH ELLERY

The news that Ellery Hanley was taking over Saints' coaching reins for the 1999 season was greeted with great anticipation by most at the club. Hanley was just what the doctor ordered! The team had been lacking discipline since mid-1997 and I believe that is why they brought Hanley in. He commanded a lot of respect from the lads; he was every player's boyhood hero because of what he had done on the rugby field, both in Britain and in Australia.

All of a sudden Ellery was here at training up at Edge Hill College, Ormskirk, coaching us with his leather jacket on over his tracksuit, with about four mobile phones going off in his pocket.

But he was good for the club and everything that the team needed, but if you had asked me at the end of the season I would have said 12 months was enough for him to do the job.

The new season got off to a bad start for me in the Challenge Cup tie at Hunslet because I got my foot caught in a tackle and it twisted around causing a very painful spiral fracture of the ankle.

I honestly thought I had snapped my leg because it was so painful. It took them three diagnoses to identify exactly what was wrong with me. My frustration was that although I saw a specialist, ankle breaks were not his particular field. They initially believed it was just a normal ankle injury and so they could not understand why it was not responding to treatment and getting any better. So I took it upon myself to try and find the top ankle specialist in England and discovered a bloke from Blackpool who had a practice in Manchester. He sent me for a bone scan, told me exactly what was wrong and what rehab I needed.

Because of that injury, I had to sit out the next cup round at Leeds where we were kicked out of the Challenge Cup as a direct consequence of our bad discipline. Ellery was not a happy coach afterwards, particularly because of the amount of penalties the team had given away. Discipline, after all, was Ellery's forte.

He gave very few penalties away as a player because his unwritten rule was, 'Get the referee in your pocket'. He had given us the tips about doing the basics, but the side did not immediately apply them. As soon as we started to listen and cut out the rubbish, and it was not rocket science, we started to go places.

Even though I could not train, I started playing again after only a five week lay-off. The course of my rehabilitation meant I could play at weekends but not train during the week. It was a gradual process, one of those where I could play at the weekend, train on Monday and then have the rest of the week off. That developed into me training on Mondays and Tuesdays and having the rest of the week off and then playing on the weekend. I reckon I probably did not train for between 12 to 15 weeks that season.

It was a tough time because we had a new coach and as club skipper I felt I needed to impress. That is the only reason I came back so early. I should have been out a lot longer because my ankle had to be set in a cast. I played in a very thin cast although I could barely get my boot on.

Things picked up once we got used to Ellery's ways of running things. He basically got hold of the players by the scruff of the neck, but it was give and take. If you did what Ellery wanted on the field, you had a bit of leeway. He was a disciplinarian who brought a lot of booze bans in, but things like that were probably needed at that time.

In enforcing those alcohol bans Ellery would say, 'There are three big games coming up. No drinking for the next three weeks'. He was very cunning, in the way he imposed that rule, because on a morning he would whisper things to you at training. What he was really doing was making you come close to his face so he could see if he could smell any whiffs of booze on your breath from the night before.

On Mondays we trained at Edge Hill where we would have a rehab pool session early in the morning. Well all the lads would generally be sat around the side of the pool, joking and talking about the antics of the weekend. Then you would see Ellery's figure approaching the doors and all of a sudden 24 bodies would dive into the pool to stop him sussing out whether we had been on the pop at the weekend.

What those bans did though, was make everybody respect each other. Subconsciously nobody wanted to be the person who let the team down. Most of the lads still used to have the odd pint or glass of wine with their wives and girlfriends, but the bans curbed the big drinking excesses.

Having said that, I remember when Ellery finally departed early the following season, all the lads were out having a day at the races. I think he must have received about 24 text messages from the lads saying, 'Ellery, we are out on the piss!'

His coaching style was not complicated, it was set out in more layman's terms in its structure. Everything was very basic and we were very fit because Nigel Ashley-Jones was our conditioner. Ellery had us perfecting the little things in rugby that make up big performances. That year it paid dividends.

At the start of that season there had been a few comings and goings. Saints had brought in massive Aussie prop Phil Adamson, who people viewed as a flop. But with Ellery, it was definitely a case of if he did not like you, it was tough. Ellery did not have the man management skills of his predecessor Shaun McCrae and if you were not in his first 17 you might as well have gone off and kicked a ball around Taylor Park. That is the hardest thing in rugby, because the players outside of the 17 are just as important because they will be called upon one day. If the coach takes a dislike to you, there is nothing you can do about it.

Ellery took an instant dislike to Adamson and ended up getting shot of him. There was all this talk about Saints signing the wrong Adamson in the first place. But the big man ended up going back to Australia, signing for Manly and I recall watching him have some top performances. So Ellery must not have been able to get the best out of him and to be fair to Adamson, he never got a chance.

Other new recruits had a more positive impact on the side. Ellery brought in three men who he knew could do a job for the team, players who he highly respected. He knew both Kevin Iro and Sonny Nickle's qualities and had seen strong running Samoan Freddie Tuilagi in action at Halifax.

Big-hitting Sonny was brought in to restore some much needed steel to our pack. He was one of those players opposing teams hated playing against, and probably filled their dressing room with dread when the words, 'Number 10, Sonny Nickle' was read from the team sheet before a game. Ellery had played alongside Kevin at Wigan during their glory days ten years previously and knew what sort of job he could do, even if 'The Beast' was at the latter end of his career.

It was strange playing alongside Kevin having watched him all those years ago – but it taught me a few things nonetheless. Kevin knew his body and how to listen to it – and I learned that too. At that stage of my career he taught me how to go a bit easier in training and save a bit. I started thinking, 'I don't get judged on how fast I run at training, but what I do on match day'. Ellery was clever in the way he trained us, because he used to leave us champing at the bit for the game and not work us too hard.

Mind you we had been flogged pre-season by Nigel Ashley Jones, but in the build-up to games we did very little and looked fresh as daisies because of that.

We got onto a good winning roll and then hit a really bad patch with a run of four defeats out of five. All of a sudden Ellery was suspended. Saints are not used to losing so many games and the first place people go looking is the coach. He is usually the first one to get it in the neck when things go wrong.

I don't know what had happened between him and the board, but the players enjoyed his style of coaching and he had the backing of the supporters too. It really hit the fan then! There were mass fan protests at the ground before, during and after the game against Hull. Even though we trounced them 74–16, over 3,000 people stayed behind singing, 'Sack the board!' and voicing their support for our suspended coach.

The players were not bothered either way, we were probably all laughing about it to be honest, but as far as we were concerned this was a private matter between the board and Hanley.

The following week Hanley was restored and we sailed through August and built some real momentum. However, we lost to Wigan in the last ever game at Central Park. Personally it was quite an experience playing there for the very last time because I had played my big schoolboy finals and watched a lot of my early rugby there.

Central Park meant a lot to me in that respect – because this was the place that had helped boost my dreams of one day becoming a professional player. I had effectively started my career there and was happy to play in the last game at the stadium.

Unfortunately, I have other reasons for remembering that day. It was a boiling hot day and I was really dehydrated afterwards. After the game I was selected for a random drug test and of course could not provide a sample immediately because of the amount of fluid I had lost in the heat of the battle so to speak. As soon as the drug tester taps you on the shoulder as you are walking off down the tunnel, he stays with you throughout until you give your sample. If you have nothing to hide, there is no problem.

Despite drinking loads of water and coffee, five hours later I still could not go. So while everybody was in the club house celebrating at 10 pm, I was sipping water by the banks of the River Douglas, chaperoned by the drugs tester, in the hope that the drink and sound of trickling water might take its effect on me!

One good thing about all the modern facilities on the new grounds these days are the special rooms that are available for such things to take place. There is a world of difference between sitting in one of those rather than a boiler room at Central Park.

For that game I had some friends up from Wales, who were staying in the hotel across the road from the ground, and I suggested they take a photograph of the famous Central Park frontage because they would not recognise it in future. When I went to see them the following day a dirty big bulldozer had already launched itself straight through the middle of it – so they got onto that job quickly.

It would have been nice to develop Wigan's new ground there, just like Widnes had done, but if you ask Andrea she is pleased to have a Tesco supermarket there because it is a lot easier than going shopping at the other side of town!

Whenever I go shopping there now I often reminisce and recall all the great games I have played in at Central Park. I think the development at the JJB Stadium has been a good thing for Wigan as a town, although I think there should be a better shrine to the rugby league tradition at the old site. I think they just have a bronze rugby ball statue tucked away near the recycling bin. They should have built something near to the middle of Tesco to symbolise it, even something similar to the statue of Brian Bevan in Warrington.

Saints finished that season in second spot behind leaders Bradford – and some pundits were already talking as if the title was on its way back to Odsal.

Our second spot was a huge improvement on the previous year's fourth placing and that meant we had home advantage in our opening play-off match, seeing off Leeds. We then travelled to Bradford in the next stage, but unfortunately the Bulls thrashed us 40–4 to go straight through to the final. Our second place finish meant we had another bite of the cherry and we accounted for Castleford in the semi. Cas were on a roll having won the first ever game of rugby league at the JJB stadium, beating hosts Wigan. Cas had good momentum, but we were on our own midden and were one step away from Old Trafford – they had no chance that night.

The Bulls had a week off ahead of the final – and this is the cause of great debate. Now for me, I would have loved to have already had our passage to the final booked and soaked up the extra week off.

But because Bradford had a very big team I reckon they could have done with having a run out to keep ticking over. The bigger team you are, the more you need to be playing and running all the time. They were at a phase where they were probably celebrating getting to Old Trafford. Where we had the one night of celebration, after beating Cas, they had the opportunity for two or three, which also probably worked in our favour.

Saints were the underdogs at Old Trafford – everybody just expected the Bulls to win. The Bullmania publicity push was in overdrive at Bradford, with the crowds up and the rest of it. I think some people thought they simply had to turn up to pick the title up against the league runners-up.

Because of that we went into that game under less pressure than previous finals – and I am not saying we had nothing to prove because we wanted to win for our speccies. But there was a lot of talk coming out of Yorkshire about avenging those Wembley losses. Everybody started reminiscing about Bradford's Challenge Cup defeats of 1996 and '97 and this was the night they were going to settle all the old scores.

The only downer for me was the circulars I kept getting prior to the game highlighting my duties and responsibilities as club captain should we win.

If I have to be interviewed I would rather it be on the spur of the moment so I don't have to think about it, that is just the way I am. But I was sent all these timetables and pieces of paper saying I had to pick my winner's ring up last, at point X in the proceedings, I have to be interviewed by Sky after the match at time Y, and at point Z I have got to address the people from the podium and so on and so forth. That last bit was a bit of a joke, because nobody could hear you on the PA because everyone was screaming and singing!

Every time I opened another envelope I kept thinking all this guff could work as a negative for me, because I was worrying more about this stuff than the actual game. They were the sort of things I did not like as captain, but I suppose I ended up getting used to them because I certainly got plenty of practice!

I got to the point where I just used to stick all that kind of stuff in my bag and not look at it because you always get somebody at the big game saying 'Chris, Sky need you there in five!' And I would say, 'OK' but then take eight minutes instead. I can be as awkward as the next man.

The atmosphere from the 50,000 plus crowd that night was absolutely tremendous and the one thing that sticks in my mind was Saints coming up with the little ploy to give us a psychological edge. Although we were playing in our blue change kit, we walked out onto the playing field wearing white tracksuit tops with a big red vee. They looked great under the floodlights and fireworks, even if the actual quality was poor. They looked the part and the club had thought that it would be nice to bring back a bit of tradition.

It was not the best night weather-wise, but we had a good feeling about it and thought our chances of winning were 50/50 and we were far from over-awed.

Even though it was a low scoring game, it was one of those incident-packed matches that everybody talks about. There was that disallowed try by Leon Pryce where their full-back Michael Withers had got his finger tips to it and knocked on. I just remember watching the slow motion repeats on the video screen in the corner of the stadium and kept thinking, 'How many more times are they going to look at this bloody thing?'

The more I looked at it, the more it began giving me doubts about my initial thoughts, so I ended up thinking, 'Withers has not touched it – they have scored!'

Saints also had three tries scrubbed off that night. Kevin Iro, a big game player if ever there was one, grabbed our critical try and Sean Long kept his composure to slot the winning conversion from out wide. To see *Saints 8 Bulls 6* flashed across the scoreboard 13 minutes from time was a sight to behold. From then it was a case of keeping at them to the final whistle.

Marvellous! People ask how we managed to win, but it was pure steel in defence. Bradford had come out like bulldozers, but we just stood up to them and hung in there. Read it in the record books, Bradford did not win that night – we did, and we deserved to.

So following a really gutsy, determined performance like that it disappointed me that we did not get the credit we deserved. I wasn't bothered about all that rubbish, was this a try, was it not? I just rejoiced in the satisfaction of running around Old Trafford to strains of 'We are the champions' on a dark autumn night, rain in the air and everybody cheering at the Saints end of the ground. That is what we play the game for.

That success was especially pleasing for me because it was my first trophy since officially becoming club captain. Even though I was confident in my own abilities as both a player and a captain, you get judged on your success with the things you win.

From my point of view it was so pleasing because I had my knockers who would say, 'Joynty does not shout at them enough!' But the people who I respected in rugby league knew that I was doing a good job not just on the field of play, but also off it, where you have to fight the lads' corner. Although you can get distracted from playing with off-the-field aspects of the job, I enjoyed that role. It was a big learning curve for me in a business sense because all of a sudden I was dealing with board members.

There were always plenty of players moaning about the win and lose bonus situation. So when I had to go in and sit down with the board I used to invite those who voiced their opinions loudest to come into the meeting with me. Well, for what their input was worth, I might as well have gone in with a few cardboard cut-outs.

Later on in my career, bonuses, under the regime of chairman Eamonn McManus and chief executive Sean McGuire, were tied up more within a business plan. Their projections are not done on a day-to-day basis. They finance the club and to run it as a successful business, you cannot suddenly incur costs half-way through the season. Good on them, because they would offer us bonuses at the start of the season. Although they may not have been enough, their job was to get the club back on a sound footing. But the beauty of that system is that all the arguments took place before the first ball had been kicked at the start of the system.

But around the 1999 season, it was a real dog fight and I can remember going into meetings two days before major games arguing the lads' case over winning bonuses. They were right old ding-dong battles I can tell you!

In the build-up to big games there would always be somebody piping up with, 'My mate plays at Wigan and they are on £x a man more for a win!'

Saints were never the best payers for Challenge Cup and Grand Final win bonuses. I have played in games where Wigan have reportedly been on £5,000 a man more to win, but you can't let that get in the way of playing. It is not half frustrating though, knowing that the blokes you are knocking down are on five grand more than you.

There used to be the old classic that used to do the rounds before big finals of, 'We'd be better off as a club, you know, if we lost this game!' And I would sit there and think, 'I am not in business, but you are talking out of your backside!' At the end of the day if you are Super League champions, Challenge Cup holders or World Club Challenge winners you think of the knock on effects and capitalise on success through marketing and sponsorship.

That Super League triumph was the first thing we had won since April '97. When we won back-to-back Challenge Cups and the first ever Super League, after such a long spell without any of the major trophies, all of a sudden we got the sweet taste of success. Then having missed a year it was important to regain that habit.

Under the format of the Grand Final, this was an extra special success. If you ask all the spectators who had seen us pick the trophy up at Old Trafford that night and collect the same trophy at Knowsley Road back in 1996, which one they preferred, every one would prefer the Old Trafford experience. It just had that extra magic.

The celebrations had barely subsided when I was off on my travels with Great Britain again. I think we only had about a week off before jetting down under for the Tri-Nations series.

It was another horrendous series defeat. We stopped at the Gold Coast, a couple of hours away from Brisbane, and the Indy 500 was on that week. We stayed in the hotel that was due to be used by members of Team GB, including British rowers Steve Redgrave and Matthew Pinsent, for the following year's Olympics. It was a magnificent hotel, with an 18-hole golf championship course. You could not ask for more in that regard, but it had been a long year on the playing front.

I did not play in the opener against the Aussies, even though I was probably in the best form of my career. Andy Farrell was Great Britain skipper and I know and respect Faz. He was batting for me to play, but I believe Iestyn Harris wanted his then Leeds team-mate Andy Hay to play. So they ended up picking Hay in the second row instead of me. I have no qualms about it, that is the coach's responsibility – but I don't think everybody owned up to their part in that decision-making afterwards.

Even though we were spoiled rotten on tour – living it up on the Gold Coast, playing golf and enjoying all the trappings of an international tourist – something was still lacking for me. This tour was not my idea of Test match rugby.

12

IT'S WIDE TO WEST

As a sportsman you strive to test yourself against the best in the world – and when those chances come along you want to make the most of them.

Unfortunately our opportunity to do that against Australia's top dogs – Melbourne Storm – in the World Club Challenge turned into something of a damp squib, it was a real non event.

The idea of the champions of Britain playing the top club from Down Under had been around since the mid 80s. I can recall standing on the packed terraces at Central Park with 37,000 others as Wigan beat Manly in 1986 in a really close, thrilling game.

But this first ever World Club Challenge of the Super League era was anything but competitive. All of a sudden last year's Grand Final win seemed light years away as we were slaughtered in a half-full JJB Stadium on a cold, wet miserable night in January.

Our preparation was really poor ahead of that evening and it just did not happen for us. On a personal note, I was really ill and had been suffering from a horrendous bout of flu all week. As a result I came off at half time and after 40 minutes I was completely shot to pieces. I ended up walking home that night, sick as a dog and totally fed up.

There had been no warm weather training in the build-up to this match – we 'prepared' for it in December and January and as a result got no real quality sessions under our belts. You don't get much in the way of quality by running around on frozen and muddy training pitches or up and down Ainsdale beach.

And the other big thing that counted against us was by the time us Great Britain lads had returned from our international duties, there was little time for us to train as a full team. By my reckoning, we probably only had around 10 days worth of training and preparation together before the Storm hit our shores.

There were also other issues to be added to the mix. New players were on the horizon, particularly Australian stand-off Darrell Trindall. Now Tommy Martyn had been one of our real stars, and he had encountered all this sort of thing some years previously when there was all the talk about Saints signing Iestyn Harris. Back then Tommy lifted his game accordingly, but this was different because they had actually fetched Trindall over.

In my view he was a kind of second rate Aussie – he was not an Andrew Johns or Brett Kimmorley – and Tommy must have thought, 'What are they playing at here?' Let's face it, if you look back, Tommy was playing some really good football, particularly around those years. He must have been gutted to think they were trying to replace him. As a person and as a player Tommy was far better. If you are going to fly somebody 12,000 miles you want somebody who is a vast improvement – and Trindall wasn't.

I reckon Tommy must have had a big grin on his face when Trindall packed his bags after playing only two matches.

Looking back, signing Trindall was not good for our set-up. Ellery had restored the discipline to the side, on and off the field, but here was a lad who had come over and become a magnet for the younger players. He had some sort of cult attraction and he was leading the young lads off the rails at a time when it had taken us a good 12 months to get them back on them!

From a captain's point of view it was hard for me, because the young lads were very impressionable at that age. Although the older players saw through Trindall, the young ones were clearly going out partying with him. The more you tried to quiz those lads about what was going on, the more you got the cold shoulder. So that more or less summed it up.

Although Trindall never had a problem with me, I only saw him in a rugby environment. He was fit and trained hard, so never gave me any problems, but I could see what he was doing to the squad, even though he only played two games.

The second of those games was the Challenge Cup clash at Headingley, where we were knocked out by Leeds for the second year running. It was really quite gutting, because we had fond memories of the Challenge Cup.

Although Ellery was still the coach you could sense the balance was all very fragile. There was clearly still tension at the club and I remember going to a sponsors' evening at the Hilton Hotel in St Helens ahead of the new season, where those differences came to the fore again. We knew the game was up really because that night Ellery really ripped into the way the club was going – it was similar to when Will Carling had a pop at the so-called 'old farts' in the hierarchy at the Rugby Football Union.

I think that was the final nail in his coffin as coach. If Saints had been winning, Ellery would have kept his job. But we had lost to Melbourne, got knocked out of the cup and then we lost to Bradford on the opening day of Super League, so that was the end of Ellery. This time there were no protests by the fans!

Ellery respected me as a player and a person. I was kind of an ace for him to play, because he knew I could do a job for him. He also brought the best out of certain players – blokes like full-back Paul Atcheson and hard working prop forward Julian O'Neill, who had an outstanding year under Hanley. Freddie Tuilagi and Kevin Iro also delivered the goods in 1999. You can ask all our guys from that year and few would have a bad word for Ellery.

On a 12-month basis you are probably looking at him as the ideal players' coach and an all-round good tactician. But because I was a little bit more mature and I also had to deal with the board in my role as captain, I probably got the story from two angles so to speak.

The other downside came with Ellery's unwillingness to talk to the press. The reporters at press conferences were not there for negative reasons, but simply to spread the rugby league gospel and reflect on our game.

Those reporters, looking for an angle to a story, would ask questions in the post-match press conference along the lines of 'Coach, I thought young Paul Wellens played well today. Do you agree?' Hanley's one line answer would be, 'They all played well!' and that would be the end of the story. He didn't feed the press anything positive.

Everything became like the secret service, so there were no

good stories coming out, particularly for the young lads who deserved the back page lead story in the *St Helens Star* that week. They never got it because Hanley would not feed the lines, so bang went their first public pats on the back.

I think the Bradford defeat was very significant in the departure of Hanley.

Bradford, of course, were still very bitter from the previous year's Grand Final because they thought the title should have been theirs. They had had all winter to dwell on that defeat and there must have been a lot of talk about owing us one.

The intense rivalry between Saints and Bradford, at this stage, was beginning to match, and even overtake, that involved in games against our more traditional foe, Wigan.

The lads used to have their own ways of dealing with those Bradford games, particularly when talking to the press. We would tend to keep quiet and not give the Bulls any ammunition to throw back at us. And if we did talk, it was always to build them up and say what a fantastic team they were.

There was always a lot of stuff coming out of Bradford and talk in the rugby papers about what they were going to do to us – and they had had this building up for five months since the Grand Final.

Although we lost that game, we always knew with Bradford that whenever it came to the crunch, we would have it over them. There was just something there, so no matter how much they talked about what was going to happen, when it came to it against us, it never did!

After Ellery had made his outburst at the sponsors' evening, I think the board probably started looking for a replacement coach straight away. But who was out there? England coach John Kear's name was mentioned – and he had done great things in the game, winning the cup with Sheffield Eagles. And then there were all the usual rumours about bringing former Australian Test centre Mal Meninga back over. The players thought we will just get on with it, and see who arrives because the decision was out of our hands.

Ian Millward was working wonders and making a name for

himself as coach of First Division Leigh. The close ties between Leigh and Saints off the field maybe smoothed the way.

Millward arrived, taking charge for our game against Hull at the Boulevard, and we went on an 11 game winning run. That first one sticks out because all of a sudden we had something new! This was just like when Shaun McCrae had taken over and brought in his new ideas in 1996. Under Millward or 'Basil' as he's known to the players, we had things like 'game sheets' and spot players became a known thing, where we would target a certain player's weaknesses. Hull had a half-back at that time who was weak in defence, so they placed one in from the wing so we couldn't get at him. Well he was our first spot player and this poor lad was sick to death of me and Newy running over him all afternoon. He would be there thinking, 'Oh, not you again'. Apparently he went up to Basil after the game and asked, 'Was I our spot player?'

All of a sudden planning for our games became interesting again and we all had a new challenge. It was always a tough game going to Hull – but I scored late on and we won easily.

We went on a great run, thumping Leeds at Headingley and scoring an Easter derby double against Wigan and Warrington.

We had some good wins at Headingley in my time – but not so many at Odsal during the Super League era. It was our bogey ground, and typically that is where our winning run ended. The Bulls completed the double over us by a single point and even though we lost 17–16, that to me was a good result because of the scars we had carried over from previous encounters there. That result gave us back some belief that we could give a good account of ourselves, even though we lost. I could not fathom it out, because we had battered Bradford many a time at Odsal in the pre-Super League era.

Apart from the odd blip, including another loss to Leeds, we also lost to Wakefield that season. Although Trinity were usually languishing in the bottom half of the table for some reason they had a good record against us. Every time Saints visited, they had that belief that they were going to turn us over.

They had the right attitude and lifted their game when they played against us, whilst I think we probably always did the opposite. The previous year they had turned us over at Oakwell, Barnsley's soccer ground. I recall being interviewed on Sky before that game. Looking back, I must have sounded really cocky, with the attitude that we are only playing Wakefield. We could not win that day even though we were going on a strong winning run.

When Millward took over as coach, he was not really aware of the significance of a Saints v Wigan game. He was oblivious to the intensity of feeling that game generates – even though he had every Tom, Dick and Harry shouting in his ear. He just prepared for it as if it was just another game. It probably took him until that heavy defeat on the last day of the season to realise the significance. Wigan were secure in first spot, with Saints in second place and we lost that final game of the league programme to them 42–4.

That defeat just did not fit in with the pattern of our previous two wins that season. It brought us all down to earth with a bang because everyone got on our case. Still we were to make amends!

Our first play-off game was against third placed Bradford in a match that will long live in the memory of anyone who was there. It was a great game with a fantastic finish – with the now immortalised 'Wide to West' try. Had we lost, we would still have had a second bite at the cherry – but after a great end-to-end game we were losing with only eight seconds on the clock.

That try is probably the one fans associate me with most, but I have only seen it twice on video since, although I have read about it a lot. It is only afterwards that I realised how little time was left on the clock. My biggest recollection is that it was late on and I was anticipating the kick. After 80 minutes of tireless effort I was shattered and thought I can't stay behind the ball, I am going to have to get on my bike. I probably scored that try that night because I was 30 yards in front of the kicker – but the ball was not kicked. I was up there on my own wondering where the ball was. I turned round to see that elaborate Harlem Globetrotters routine going on.

I think everybody had a hand in that, Longy kicked it across to Kevin Iro, who passed it back to Steve Hall. He managed to offload to Sean 'Choppy' Hoppe on the inside who found Longy again. It came across the line and Westy beat some good men, showing some good skill before getting the ball out to me. I could see Jimmy Lowes coming across, but I knew I had the legs on him.

Sully was screaming encouragement on my shoulder but there was no need to pass because there was no full-back in front of me and Jimmy Lowes would have had to have done a Superman dive to stop me. It was a special try and the ground just erupted. It just went absolutely mad, everybody was jumping on top of me and Longy ran up and ripped St Bernard's head off and started running round with it! It probably shattered a few poor kids' illusions when it dawned on them that our cuddly mascot is just a bloke with a bald head and a beard! It was like telling them that Father Christmas did not exist.

It was all too much for Bradford coach, Matthew Elliott, who fell off his seat in the stand. It was not just any old try. It was so significant, although it never became try of the season – they were probably all Yorkshire men picking that award!

That try probably put a marker down to show Saints are a side that never knows when we are beaten. That tag stayed – even through to 2004 – and teams leading us used to think, 'Bloody hell, they are coming back!' That was the sort of mentality that took us forward as a team because we literally had that 'never say die' attitude. And as if to underline it, there would always be a reference back to that night. You would hear, 'Do you remember that try Joynty scored in the final second of the game!' If you are four points down, it gives you that confidence not to panic, but to keep playing and stick to your guns. It also filled the opposition with dread of, 'We have not won this yet!'

What this Bradford game gave us was belief in ourselves. We had that big element of lady luck because you could not set that final move up on the training ground. Even with no defenders in front of you, no matter how many times you attempted to imitate that, if you tried to mock it up, you would never be able to. When we all sat in the dressing room after that we had that feeling that somebody was definitely on our side – and the following week we went to Wigan and blew them out of the water, 54–16, to march through to the final.

Our momentum was building and Anthony Sullivan crowned a great night by scoring that beauty of a full-length try from his line.

There was no finer sight in this game than Sully in full flight! He was quick and he was part of that left hand side gang of Tommy, myself, Newy and Sully who worked great together. Sully was one of those wingers who would always take half a chance on the outside and most of the time he would get there.

Getting to the Grand Final at this stage was in contrast to the previous year – this time it was our turn to have the week off in between events. It was a good feeling to know we were on our way. It had been a long year and I suppose we were glad of the break. We celebrated getting to the final, but then knuckled down to preparing for it straight away. We were not on the ale for a week. We trained as if we were playing the weekend of the semi-final – simulating a game in training in four 20-minute quarters.

We just wanted to get a game under our belts to keep ticking over – there was contact, without it being full tackle, which was the intention. We didn't want any injuries ahead of a Saints v Wigan Grand Final

Personally I was just enthused by the training, and could not wait to get to this game. When you are playing well you can't wait for next game to come along. We had to wait 15 days and were champing at the bit for a game.

I was quite relaxed when I was interviewed by Sky and I remember Faz looking at me during the interview as if to think, 'He is calm about this'. Unusually I enjoyed talking to the television people and Faz must have thought I was on something because I was chatting away like nobody's business. Mind you, they never did show it on television.

I could not wait for the first whistle to come. And my parents, who don't come and watch me, but had gone to the final in 1999 had turned up for this one too.

Getting to the game was not without incident. We went straight to Old Trafford after meeting up at the club, where we got a new tie and a flower. It was like going to Salford, rather than a big final. The coach then got a police escort on the M602. There was a police Range Rover parked up on the hard shoulder and so our driver assumed that this was our escort and pulled over. But they waved us away and knew nothing about it. It was a genuine mistake and when we got back on the motorway we saw the police motorcycle outriders up ahead.

But the next thing we knew was the previous policemen from the Range Rover pulled us up for going onto the hard shoulder. All the lads were nervous and there was this copper pacing in front of the coach booking the driver. He must have been a Wigan fan!

The game went really well for the team and me personally. Wigan had swapped things around a bit and put Kris Radlinski into the centre and Jason Robinson, playing his last game of rugby league, at full-back. I always found Robinson more dangerous from full-back because he was very elusive. You could never get hold of him or really get a shot on him. Usually you tried to just get a hand on him to slow him down because he was that quick. I had played a lot of rugby with him for Great Britain and England and against him. It was a shame to see him go because he was hot property and a fantastic player. It was a loss to our game when he went.

We got off to a fine start and early on we broke down the left and I flicked the ball out of the tackle to set up our first try for Sean Hoppe. Even on slow motion you can't see the ball coming out, but all of a sudden Choppy is going over in the corner! I thought, 'This is what we want'.

We took a decent 17–4 lead. I scored two tries – I barged over for one and then Longy cut through and sent me under the sticks for the other.

Then Wigan clawed their way back to within a point at 17–16. Again, Old Trafford does tire you out – it does sap you. We managed to hang on in there. Everybody played well and I remember Longy cutting down their experienced Aussie Test centre Steve Renouf a few times.

Then Freddie Tuilagi, playing his final game for Saints, took Tommy Martyn's superb long pass to fly in at the corner. Longy banged the conversion over from the touchline to put it beyond reach. And then just to add the icing on the cake, my young second row partner Tim Jonkers finished off the scoring with a great try.

Timmy was a local lad, a former Blackbrook Royals player, who would train the house down. To me he was another Phil Clarke in the making. Even though there was nothing spectacular in his game, you could always count on him.

We had another youngster, John Stankevitch, on the bench also and that paid dividends in years to come because those lads had been playing in big games from an early age. People think Timmy is a veteran now when in fact he is only 23, mind you those same folk think I am 48 because I have been around so long.

It was just unfortunate for Timmy that he had all those injuries. Nobody trains as hard as Timmy. He is such a disciplined lad that in a couple of years time he will make his mark on the game. I think he is a future Great Britain star because the form he showed between 1999 and 2001 underlines that. He just needs a bit of luck.

He broke his ankle when he was playing hooker against Leeds in 2001 and everyone could see he had gone, but he stayed on the field, which probably made his injury worse. Timmy was such a game lad and was keen to carry on, but the severity of his injury at that time was a big blow. He might have been picked in the Great Britain squad that year – that is how well he was playing. Now I bet he wished he had stuck his hand up at that game and said, 'I have had enough!'

That Grand Final winning team had the lot – blend of speed, craft and a lot of steel in the pack. There was a good combination of youth and experience and everyone complemented each other.

That was the swansong for Apollo, Freddie Tuilagi and Julian O'Neill, which made it extra special. To this day I really don't know why they got rid of prop Julian O'Neill. The game was crying out for good front rowers and here was a lad who was young, who went on to serve Wakefield and Widnes well.

Julian was a bit like me and I knew the work he was putting in. He was undervalued as a prop and you only noticed what he did when he was not out there. I have a lot of time for him as a player and a bloke because he was a workhorse who did his job well. They said he suffered with his lateral footwork and there is talk about multi-skilling. But that is not what being a good prop forward is all about – you always need players to take some of the heat off. Maybe he did not have all the attributes, but he certainly did a job that was needed 30 years ago and is still needed in the modern-day game.

Choppy was great with regards to the professionalism he showed and his clean-cut image. He was highly respected among the lads. He was a fit lad, and great to have around the club. He is just one of those good blokes.

To beat Wigan was even better than turning Bradford over the previous year. We were not sick of beating Bradford yet, mind you – but there was history to this battle. We could have played it on Taylor Park or Robin Park and it would have been sweet. But at Old Trafford, the Theatre of Dreams, you just can't beat it.

Beating Wigan was great – especially as it is my home town. When you go down to the newsagent's after a game you always get a few wisecracks, but it is water off a duck's back. It is always pleasing when we have done them again, especially if I had a major contribution in their downfall.

I won the Harry Sunderland Trophy that night – seven years after winning it for the first time against Wigan in 1993. It was good smirking tackle to take home and good for my parents and family. I heard the award being announced over the tannoy six minutes from time and it was pleasing, particularly as we were going to win the game.

Winning it a second time, so long after the first one, shows a level of consistency on my part. When I took the award home the second time to my mam and dad's house it became a bit of a talking point. 'Do you remember last time it was here on top of the telly?' they would say.

It was so good to win it in '93, but even better in 2000 because of the time difference. I was playing well, not many second rowers have won that – it is usually a half-back or a three-quarter that walks off with that award.

Although I have won a few man of the match awards in my time, the one that has really eluded me is the Lance Todd Trophy given during the Challenge Cup Finals. That, along with failing to win an Ashes series, are the big disappointments in my career.

Me alongside the other Wigan lads selected to play for England Schoolboys in 1987.

Me in August 1991 just before the start of my last season at Oldham.

Attempting to fend off a Halifax tackle in my Oldham days.

Making a break, with Oldham colleague Richard Pachniuk up in support.

I never liked that blue striped kit – but it did not stop us beating Widnes to make it through to Wembley for the 1996 Challenge Cup Final.

The 1996 Challenge Cup post match celebrations were marked by the wearing of some unusual head gear!

Taking the ball up against London in that crucial Super League clash at The Valley in 1996.

Saints are crowned inaugural Super League champions after thrashing Warrington at Knowsley Road on the last day of the season in 1996.

Looking to pick out a runner with a long ball at Headingley in 1999.

Looking to get the ball out of the tackle in the league game against Hull in 1998. Former team-mate Alan Hunte looks on.

Champions again! The scene in the Old Trafford changing rooms after the epic 1999 Grand Final win over Bradford.

That famous, but crucial, last second 'Wide to West' try in the 2000 play off game against Bradford! I will never live this one down – and it has been picked out as many fans' favourite all time score.

Picking up the Harry Sunderland Trophy for the second time was a proud moment for me. I previously won the award back in 1993 for my man of the match display in the Premiership Final, which was also against Wigan.

Going over for one of my brace of tries against Wigan at Old Trafford in 2000.

Picking up the Super League trophy after beating Wigan in 2000.

Jubilation! There is no greater feeling than beating Wigan – particularly at Old Trafford. We were certainly jubilant after that 2000 Grand Final win.

Parading the 2000 Super League title with vice-captain Paul Sculthorpe.

The Saints team gathers for their most intensive pre-season training ever at Lanzarote in January 2001.

Lifting the World Club Challenge trophy in 2001 with Tommy Martyn and Ian Millward.

Top of the world! The team celebrates our World Club Challenge win at the Reebok. Nobody gave us a chance, but we proved them all wrong.

Going over for that crucial match-levelling try against Brisbane after taking the last pass from Paul Newlove. The conditions at that stage were atrocious.

Celebrating the World Club Challenge win over Brisbane with Keiron Cunningham and Paul Newlove.

Celebrating our semi-final Challenge Cup win over Leeds in 2001 with Keiron Cunningham and Sean Long.

The Twickenham final against Bradford in 2001 was a tight, intense game. Here I get the ball out of the tackle to offload to Sean Long.

Completing the treble! Saints celebrate after beating Bradford Bulls in the 2001 Challenge Cup Final at Twickenham.

Taking the ball up against the Aussies in the 2001 First Test at the McAlpine Stadium.

Treble tops! Me with the Challenge Cup, World Club Challenge Trophy and the Super League Trophy after winning all three in just over six months.

Me and Scully celebrate winning the First Test against the Aussies at Huddersfield in 2001. Our joy was short lived and we lost the series 2-1 with defeats at Bolton and Wigan.

Me, with fellow Saints players Paul Wellens and Paul Sculthorpe at the JJB, Wigan following the shattering Third Test defeat in 2001. With that loss went my last chance of ever winning the Ashes.

Getting the ball around Leeds' winger Mark Calderwood in that emphatic Challenge Cup semi-final win in 2002.

Lifting the Super League title again after that late win over the Bulls in 2002. Paul Wellens is pictured in the background sporting the fractured cheekbone that forced him to miss most of the game.

Me and my mate Paul Newlove with the Super League trophy after securing the win in 2002.

We were joined in our celebrations after the 2002 Grand Final by the didgeridoo player who performed before the game.

We've done it! Our first Challenge Cup Final triumph over Wigan since 1966 went down quite well! Despite the 32-16 scoreline, it was quite a close, intense game.

Former Saints, Wales and British Lions centre Scott Gibbs was a welcome guest at the Millennium Stadium for our 2004 victory over Wigan. It was also my daughter Megan's first game!

In 1997 I had a very good chance of winning it, but still don't know what the score was when they totted it up. I am not regarded as a great player, but I have proved that I can perform on the big occasion. That is something you have in you – I suppose I have just been consistent. When it comes to awards I have found that a consistent player always has to do something more spectacular than somebody who plays well in a one-off game.

13

ANSWERING IRELAND'S CALL ... TO THE BAR!

I had become increasingly disillusioned with my international career with England and Great Britain and to be honest I just wanted to pack it in. My thinking on the matter was, 'Why should I, after a tough domestic season, go into an environment I am not enjoying?'

But then it took a bit of a twist prior to the 2000 World Cup – helped along the way by the persuasiveness of Great Britain props Terry O'Connor and Barrie McDermott. They had already opted to wear the green of Ireland for that tournament and knowing my Celtic roots said, 'Come and play for us, Joynty!'

So I weighed it up and thought, 'Why not? I will go for it and see if I can get a bit of my hunger back'.

As far as I was concerned, I was in my pomp as a player and easily in the reckoning for England honours again that year. It was not true that I had earlier asked the England coach for a guaranteed starting spot, I have no idea who started that story. I had been around long enough to know nobody is guaranteed a spot in rugby league, no matter what your name is. England had already approached me and told me that they were going to America to prepare for the tournament and set out what they were doing.

But I opted for Ireland and I think they tried to make it difficult because they wanted to know the background to my Irish roots and more or less told me to prove it. There are a lot of Irish descendants in Wigan and St Helens – you only have to look at a phone book or down a list of lads' names on a team sheet.

I had to get copies of both my nan's and mum's birth

certificates, which was no problem. My mum had the lot – I even had my great grandmother's birth certificate so there was no question of not being able to prove there was Irish in me. My nan was born in a little place called Belmullet in County Mayo, tucked into the west coast of Ireland

A couple of us got a bit of stick and there was all this talk like, 'You are only playing for Ireland because of all that Guinness you have supped!'

Some of the critics might have had a case when saying because we had already played for England, it was maybe devaluing the international jerseys by going elsewhere. But I think it also showed that there was a problem with the international game in that people were not enjoying it. Why else would Terry O'Connor, Gary Connolly and I have opted not to play for England?

That is no disrespect to Ireland and I believe I made the right decision.

The 2000 World Cup followed more or less straight on from the Super League Grand Final. We had to fly off to La Manga the Monday after the Old Trafford victory for the Ireland squad's warm weather training/booze up! That latter part was more what it was all about and to be honest I was probably still drunk from the Grand Final celebrations. I must have been because I forgot my passport – so I had to borrow a car to race back home to Wigan to pick it up.

We had a great gang of lads and we used to train hard during the day leading up to match days and we had a great team spirit, which cost nothing. We kept hearing about how the England lads' trip to America had cost big bucks, yet we were in a little pub in Belfast with the stout flowing, fiddle playing and songs going – money could not buy the craic we were having.

I roomed with Kevin Campion, who was playing for Brisbane Broncos at the time. We all got on as a team should get on – we got quite close over those six weeks and were out boozing every night apart from the days before a game. We spent a week in Belfast and a couple of weeks in Dublin and I think we saw off more than a few barrels of the black stuff between us.

It was a good trip – led by coaches Steve O'Neill and Andy Kelly, with Ralph Rimmer as the manager. They were charged with doing with us what Jack Charlton had done to the Republic of Ireland soccer team in the late 80s. A lot of that soccer side that did well in the 1990 World Cup were not born in Ireland either. When I agreed to play for Ireland, the first thing I received in the post was a CD of 'Ireland's Call!' which was the anthem we sang before the game.

We used to sing it with such gusto and there was a real togetherness there for all to see. If you thought the rendition before kick-off was raucous, you should have heard the one after last orders. Whichever pub we were in, we would always finish off with a rendition of 'Ireland's Call' after we had supped up.

I was already acquainted with a lot of the lads in the camp and knew former Warrington and Oldham half-back Martin Crompton because he was a Wigan lad. I got to know him better with the Ireland set-up. We became good pals on that trip. Crommy had just come back from a knee operation so he did not play in the tournament, but he still held the record for consecutive nights out on the ale! I think he did 39 out of 42. Even though we were boozing regularly we got the job done. We needed to because we had a tough group with Scotland, Samoa and the New Zealand Maoris in there.

We kicked off the tournament at Windsor Park, Belfast, and I had the honour of scoring the opening try of the World Cup, after only two minutes, in our 30–16 win over Samoa. Ireland's line-up that day was not bad: Steve Prescott; Brian Carney, Michael Withers, Michael Eagar, Mark Forster; Tommy Martyn, Ryan Sheridan; Terry O'Connor, Danny Williams, Barrie McDermott, Chris Joynt, Kevin Campion, Luke Ricketson. A crowd of 3,000 turned out for that game, but only 1700 turned up the following week at Tolka Park, Dublin for our 18–6 win over Scotland.

We finished the group unbeaten, accounting for the Maoris 30–16 in the last group game. To underline our achievement the Maori side that day included Clinton Toopi, Toa Kohe-Love, David Kidwell, Sean Hoppe, Gene Ngamu, Tawera Nikau and Martin Moana.

We won all of our group games and we took a good following over with us. I reckon about 40 came over from Wigan, including my brother and my mate Winny, and they had a laugh. If we hadn't had our fill of the black stuff already, they arranged a guided tour round the Guinness brewery for us. What a great trip that was!

Ireland at that time had built something special, but there were never enough regular fixtures to build on what had been created in that tournament. We got loads of interest over there and did plenty of interviews, and the BBC made a bit of a fuss of it. We went all over the place while we were there and when we were in Northern Ireland, we went down the Garvaghy Road, which was a flashpoint of the Troubles at the time. When we stayed in Belfast we had a brilliant time. It was a great city and it gets a bad reputation, so I was pleasantly surprised.

It did have its funny sides mind – we were drinking in this club in the city one night when the DJ turned the music off and said, 'There has been a coded bomb warning issued, please vacate the club'. Well I was up and ready to leave, but Crommy was still sat there supping his beer not prepared to budge an inch. He said, 'I'm not leaving! They did this last night when I'd only just got the ale in and by the time I got back my pint had been mine-swept!' Much as I am fond of the odd pint, I shook my head and said, 'Well I'm not taking any chances for a pint, I'll see you outside!'

Finishing top of the group meant we played England in the quarter finals at Headingley. It sounds mad, but we were not bothered about the England set-up and how they had got on. We just carried on what we were doing and we were well up for that game. We thought, 'This will be superb if we can turn them over!' And looking at the quality team we had, there was no reason why we couldn't give it to them.

Our lads had nothing to prove, but we were excited about the possibility of chucking a cat among the pigeons. The authorities made it harder for us, I reckon, because I think the last thing they wanted was us beating the hosts! The accommodation they put us in before that game was a right hole 30 miles away from Headingley in South Yorkshire. The lads nicknamed the hotel a mental hospital, because that is what it felt like. It had a disinfectant smell to it like a hospital. Still it didn't bother us, those lads who had opted to play for Ireland wanted to play for Ireland.

It was a close game, but England eventually ran away with it at the end beating us 26–16. Maybe it was a game too far because it had been a long hard season for all of us, and we had been on the pop for a month!

The World Cup itself was a bit of a disaster. There were very few tickets sold and games were all over the place in mad parts of the country like Northampton and Gloucester. Don't get me wrong; I am all for expansion, but it did not do much for the crowds. To make matters worse, there were a load of train disruptions and the weather was appalling. It was the wettest November in years.

On the other side of the coin it was one of the best six weeks of my international career with regards to getting together a gang of lads who enjoyed what they are doing. There was none of this regimented POW camp stuff like seeing a sports psychologist, boring meetings and three-hour video review sessions. What we did was enjoy each other's company and play when we needed to. We had the best of both worlds, enjoying the trappings of full-time professionalism, but acting like we did when we were part-timers in the old days!

I think what happened after we got knocked out summed up the bizarre nature of some of our japes! We had been drinking around Sheffield and after leaving a club we jumped into a taxi. One of the lads said to the driver, 'Excuse me mate, but didn't the Yorkshire Ripper finally get caught around here?'

Now some folk might have taken that the wrong way or thought it a strange query. But the driver spun the car round and then began taking us on an impromptu crime trail. He took us past a park and up a dead end to show us the spot where Peter Sutcliffe was arrested. And then he pulled up at the spot where the Ripper had hidden his hammer. He was revelling in his job as a grisly tour guide and drove us around for about an hour. He dropped us off at the hotel and me and Kevin Campion were thinking it was going to cost us a fortune, but the driver only asked for £3.

The following day involved a lot of unplanned drinking and some long good-byes.

The coach was supposed to be leaving the hotel at 9.30am so I told Andrea to pick me up at the Haydock Thistle at 11.30. I rang back at 11.15am to tell her to leave it for a couple of hours because we hadn't left yet! By accident, it just turned into one last big session. When we dropped somebody off in Leeds, we had a few more there – it would have been rude not to really – it was a really great way to round off, finishing off the way we started! We all arrived home worse for wear and 12 hours late. But what a great experience!

14

TOP OF THE WORLD!

The fact that Saints had a lot of players on World Cup duty, playing for England, Ireland, Scotland, Wales and the Cook Islands meant we only really had a pre-season of barely six weeks before we were back into it big time.

The formidable figures of the Brisbane Broncos were looming on the horizon and we were determined to have a proper crack at the World Club Championship this time.

We had learned so much from the Melbourne Storm defeat the previous year. And because we had Brisbane in our sights, the intensity of the training was a month ahead of our normal schedule. That was speeded up further by going to Lanzarote – the place that has now become an annual pilgrimage for many sports teams. Sport is very competitive, so if one team finds a good place, everybody fights to get over there the following year. The key weeks are very highly sought after. I reckon it is all a bit of a fad really – but what you get over there is quality training. You can spend more time on a training field because you are not ankle deep in mud or being frozen off. Not only was it a case of the weather being fine, but we were also surrounded by fit people. Club La Santa, where we were staying, is designed for athletes and wherever you went reminded you of that. People there were not stuffing pies and burgers in their faces, put it that way – all the meals were healthy. You were in an environment where you had the likes of Estonia's Olympic gold medal winning decathlete Erki Nool running round. All our lads used to be in awe of the bloke because he had the sort of physique on him that looked as though somebody had walked up to him and chiselled it out. There were all kinds of sports people there – everybody was a professional.

This might sound daft, but personally I would sooner stop at home, but that whole experience was very intense. Our preparation was a weapon in our armoury and much better than ploughing through the sand on Ainsdale beach.

When we got there it was anything but a holiday camp, and I think all the players kind of knew that something special was about to happen that year. The commitment and attitude was absolutely there 110 per cent. We were focused on match-related stuff a month earlier than normal – usually it would have just been fitness we were working on. We just had Brisbane Broncos in our sights and Millward's assistant, Harry Bryant, had done his homework in preparing us to smash that target. It was probably one of the most intense week's training I have ever undertaken.

Saints had been written off after the previous year's disappointing performance and when we got to the big press call in the week building up to it with Brisbane players like Darren Lockyer and Gordon Tallis, we were thinking, 'Hey up, we're up against it again'. I actually found some of the press conferences to be quite negative, and a lot of people there were almost in awe of the Broncos. It seemed that a lot of the press men would sooner talk to the Brisbane lads than to some of us lot. I am not sure if it was the novelty factor or whether they were thinking they could talk to us 51 weeks of the year.

I maintain to this day that when we walked out at the Reebok, only about 22 people really knew that something special was going to happen that night. Nobody gave us a chance. We knew something amazing was on the cards because of our training. We were flying!

Rugby league needed a shot in the arm because the World Cup had been such a wash-out with England getting stuffed by New Zealand in the semi-finals. We had gone from being the second best nation to a poor third.

The game plan we had was not based on rocket science. Once again there were little things we did well. One of those things was pinning Wendell Sailor down, because he was one of those players who would try to fight you all the time. We knew how quick a team they were at playing the ball and building momentum, so every time I got hold of Sailor he would want to maul and grapple with me because he had that aggression. I had a ploy of gripping him and winding him up even more, knowing full well he would want to fight me and the result would be he would have the slowest play the ball on the park and our lads could get the line set.

They were pretty fierce opening exchanges and Brisbane got off to a decent start. They scored first through stand-off Shaun Berrigan after seven minutes, but we hung in there and a Paul Sculthorpe try pegged it back midway through the first half. Tries from Philip Lee and Brad Meyer pushed the Broncos 18–6 up but we refused to bow down. In a really memorable night, the things that stick out most for me were Longy taking a pass off me to go over for the try which raised our spirits.

The other big thing was the hailstones because when they started coming down Sailor turned to me and said, 'What the bloody hell is this, Joynty?' and in my best Wigan accent I said, 'I think they're called hailstones!' At that stage I thought to myself, these fellas don't like this. They were used to swanning round Brisbane and that was a big factor in swinging the game.

The hailstorm was the cue for our match-levelling try. It was down my favoured left flank, Newy had gone through but he gave me an absolute shocker of a pass, which I had to reach around for. It was something me and him had probably done a hundred times before, but usually it was Newy crossing, not me. I tucked it under my arm and then it was a clear run to the line, then next thing big Gordon Tallis came in late with the knees as I touched down. It winded me, but I was not bothered because I knew I had got the all-important score. That was a kind of frustration on their part, because even though there was quite a bit of time to play, they knew we had more or less got them. It was just a case of holding on for us then. The sight of those boys from the sunshine state standing behind the posts, getting lashed in the face by a Horwich hailstorm was a big boost for us. The rest is history as they say. We knew they could score from anywhere – but that surge never came. I reckon that was testimony to our fitness and determination.

Scully and Longy banged over a couple of drop goals to put us in front and that is how it finished: Saints 20 Brisbane 18! They gave me the man of the match award but there must have been loads of other candidates. I just think I got it for scoring the crucial try at the turning point. Personally I would have given the award to Paul Sculthorpe that night because he was tireless in attack and defence. But once again it was probably the tries and breaks syndrome coming through from the judges, but I am not complaining.

Everybody has their own lasting memory of that game, whether it is the image of Paul Wellens playing virtually the full 80 minutes with his shattered eye socket; or the performances of Keiron Cunningham and new Aussie recruit David Fairleigh, who were awesome that night.

The crowd was a touch disappointing and I reckon those who did not go were absolutely gutted. Those who made the trip, well you have to take your hat, gloves and scarves off to them.

The only other disappointment was Chris Caisley, the Super League chairman, who didn't look too pleased with our victory. I don't know what that was about.

But that win left a lasting mark on the town – as you drive in from Haydock, Rainhill, Newton, Rainford or Prescot you still see the sign, 'Welcome to St Helens, Home of the 2001 World Club Champions!' That was not something we would have predicted in 1997 when we were getting thumped all over the place by all the Aussies in the World Championship.

World crown or not, we had no time to rest on our laurels, because we drew Wigan in the opening round of the Challenge Cup. It had done us a favour really and because we were match hardened, we had it over Wigan and we were ready for them more than ever. We had hit the ground running because our preparation was so far ahead. We did not specifically target winning the Challenge Cup at the expense of everything else, because you can't drop points in the league. We had to keep both competitions up in the air.

Our reward for beating Wigan was an away tie at Whitehaven in the next round and coach Ian Millward rested a few of our first teamers. The likes of Sean Hoppe, Kevin Iro, Sean Long, David Fairleigh, Keiron Cunningham, Peter Shiels and Paul Sculthorpe all sat this one out.

It was a little bit blasé and almost as if we were taking automatic victory for granted. We ended up booking into a hotel a couple of miles away from the Recreation Ground. Well we knew the dressing sheds were abysmal at Whitehaven so we got changed at the hotel. We rolled up 20 minutes before the game with our trackies on and all these mad keen Cumbrians or Marra men, were giving it to us as we got off the coach. They were bawling, 'Look at these posing, cocky bastards!' You could see the intensity of feeling and the crowd gave us plenty of flak as we were warming up. We didn't play well at all and to cap it all Vila Matautia got sent off.

Vila was knackered and I made a sign to the bench to take him off, because it had got to the point where I knew he was going to start giving penalties away. It took him three rucks to get back onside and on his way back he got in somebody's way and ended up clocking them. It is what happens when you get tired – you start swinging arms!

One of the funnier things in that game was Newy's problem with an advertising hoarding! We were playing in black and there was a black advertising hoarding on the touchline and I think Newy must have thrown three passes to that board because he could see it out of the corner of his eye and thought it was Sully.

The Cumbrians gave us one hell of a game and it must have spurred them because they were thinking, 'Scully isn't there, Longy is not playing!' They had a bit of a sniff of a shock. I don't think Ian Millward understood the Challenge Cup, the way it was steeped in tradition and no second chances. He must have thought 'Second division Whitehaven, I will rest a few here!' Joking aside, I don't think he has learned since.

Our opening Super League game that season was frozen off on the first Friday at Valley Parade. It affected us big time, because we were preparing to play and still didn't know whether it would be on the Sunday. In my opinion it should not have been played because the ground was still rock hard in parts. You don't mind hard summer pitches, but if you imagine putting your boot into the turf and then it freezes, that is a lot more dangerous. The pitch at Bradford was of a good standard, but you just need a rut in the ground to come a cropper. They won 31–24. It was a close game and Robbie Paul gave an outrageous dummy and scored in the corner, which was an horrendous try to concede.

We went onwards and upwards after that going through to the

Challenge Cup semi-final date with Leeds at the JJB stadium. It was nip and tuck all the way through in what was an outstanding game. We won – we were on a good run at the JJB having won there in the play-offs against Wigan. We were having a good spell there but it changed later on in my career.

That semi-final win put us through to Twickenham where once again Bradford were the opposition.

The work on rebuilding Wembley was under way so this was the second year they had taken the final on the road so to speak after playing at Murrayfield the previous year. I was not impressed with Twickenham – it didn't float my boat venue-wise and a few of the speccies probably agreed.

It was not the prettiest of games – although I have watched the video of the match a few times and there was some magnificent defence in there from all of us. My tackle sheet read 35, and there were plenty of others with high stats too. It was one of those rare times that you even see Newy coming in with the shoulder. Everybody kind of got stuck in and they never crossed our line.

We went there to do a job and it was done efficiently and with the minimum of fuss. Our half-backs Tommy and Longy were at their telepathic best, and put the Paul brothers into the shade that day. Appropriately, at the home of kicking all our tries came from the boot, with angled grubbers paying off for Tommy and Keiron Cunningham to touch down.

We knew how to handle Bradford's dominant pack – particularly their awesome foursome. They were used to beating everybody in 20–25 minutes so the longer you held them out, the greater were your chances because they kind of ran out of ideas when they were not barnstorming through. It was just a case of staying with them. They were the Challenge Cup holders having beaten Leeds the previous year after bombing the living daylights out of Leeds winger Leroy Rivett.

Everybody had predicted that Henry Paul would do the same with Anthony Sullivan, who had had a rare off day with the high kicks the week before the Cup Final at Warrington. That Warrington match was a one-off game really, and Newy had also been sent off for a high tackle. It was not a big issue with Sully dropping those balls. This thing happens in rugby, one week you have a shocker, the next a blinder. It is just highlighted more on the wing, especially when it's being televised.

Sully was a confidence player and he will admit that himself. Millward knew that and good on him for sticking by Sully during what must have been a difficult week. It was early on in the year and if Millward had not picked him, Sully's confidence would have been done for months afterwards. Millward stuck by him not out of loyalty, sympathy or sentiment, but because he knew Sully was a match winner and against a big side like Bradford, if you gave him half a yard it was try time.

It is not that putting high kicks up to Sully did not cross Bradford's mind – especially as it had worked so effectively in the past. But they were not allowed to launch an aerial attack that day because we had such a really good kicking game ourselves. That meant they were bringing it off their own line all the time, so they never really had any opportunity to launch attacking kicks. They just had to settle on ones where they were trying to pin us back a bit further. Victory was a testament to our defensive resolve and our tactical nous.

To sum up the day – the weather was poor, the ground was rubbish but at least the win made it worth our while.

Although Newy had been sent off the week before the final for a high tackle, I don't think there was much danger of him being suspended, particularly for a first offence. He followed me up the steps to take the cup from Prime Minister Tony Blair. The PM muttered something to me, but I don't recall what was said really – all I was thinking was this was three trophies in the bag – a unique treble.

The week following the Cup Final saw us get a 74-point drubbing at Leeds. I don't think anybody was that bothered – we had been on the lash for a fair few days. If you can't have a drink after completing a treble, when can you?

Once we knuckled down we carried on winning, but bit by bit the treble winning team began to fall apart, which made our tilt at the Super League even tougher. Longy copped a late challenge from Brandon Costin at Huddersfield at the end of May. As a tackler it is hard to pull yourself out of tackles like that when you are challenging a kicker and wanting to put pressure on him. But from the kicker's point of view, if you only have one leg on the floor when you take the hit, it is very dangerous.

I am sure there was no intent on Costin's part. I have seen tackles when they have come in two seconds late and thought, 'You dirty swine!' I know it was a bitter blow for us. It put Longy out for the rest of the season and he needed a major knee reconstruction. Because of the sort of player Longy is, this was a massive blow, particularly as there was not much available to fill in.

Coach Ian Millward ended up tinkering with the team, adjusting his troops, putting Wello up to scrum half, which then impacted elsewhere in the side. There was not enough time to try too many different things. And then Newy got snipered going for the line at Hull, tearing his Achilles.

It was bad enough losing our creator and kicker in Longy, but to then lose our most prolific try scorer in Newy was another bitter blow. Then before the year was up Sully heard we had signed Darren Albert for the following year, so he decided to take an early opportunity to leave and make a few bob in Wales playing rugby union for Cardiff. It turned out OK for him because he got international honours for Wales A, which is probably something he had wanted to do.

I was sorry to see Sully go – he was our longest serving player at the time – a title that then went over to me!

Losing those players affected the team, but also my own game given the relationship I had with Newy and Sully down that left hand side. The team gets shuffled around. And it is a case of sticking in and carrying on. With injuries, however, I always look on the bright side because it gives somebody else a chance. Unfortunately, we just didn't have sufficient quality coming through.

The situation got worse, because we then lost Sonny Nickle after he copped a six-month ban after his heavy tackle broke Leeds hooker Robbie Mears' jaw. In the same game, David Fairleigh badly damaged his shoulder. The big Aussie prop had been a real rock for us all season and had recently signed an extension to his contract to stay the following year. He couldn't train properly for weeks and I think because his injury was so bad he decided to go back on his decision to stay on another year. Although they patched him up for the end of season games, he was not the same player.

He was arguably one of the best imported players Saints have ever had, but he could not play with that shoulder and he had no hit left in him. He was a massive loss to us. When you lose forwards of the calibre of Sonny Nickle and David Fairleigh it becomes tough work. But there is always a silver lining, and opportunities knocked for young hooker Jock McConnell, who scored a hat-trick on his debut against Cas. He was a local lad who did well for us when given the chance.

Saints limped into the play-offs and travelled to the Boulevard to play Hull with Fairleigh well patched up to the extent that he should not have played. Hull's England international prop Paul Broadbent ran at him straight away and Fairleigh's shoulder copped the worst of it.

I was in the wars myself that night, because Vila Matuatia accidentally knocked me out. We were going into a tackle together and all of a sudden his big paw came over the top and clonked me. When I hit the deck our physio Clare Mannion came on and said, 'Where are you, Joynty?'

'Hull,' I said.

'Which Hull?'

'Hull Hull, not Hull KR!'

I saw stars and went off for a couple of minutes, but went straight back on.

However, I suffered delayed concussion and had problems for a month after that and was slurring my words like a drunk.

Head injuries are taken very seriously these days, because as a player you are that keen to get on. When I first started playing, assessment was quite primitive and always a case of, 'How many fingers have I got up?' Nowadays if you get knocked out, you have computerised head checks in which they compare your responses to questions.

The game at Hull was quite a roller-coaster ride because we took a big 20–6 lead. Hull came storming back to equalise and the packed Boulevard crowd was in full voice with their anthem 'Old Faithful' being bellowed out from what was left of the old

Threepenny Stand. Once again Tommy was on hand to win yet another game for us late in the day, but to be honest our lads were shattered.

We went to Wigan for the final eliminator, but it was a game too far. We were slaughtered at the JJB and David Fairleigh, Vila Matautia, Kevin Iro and Steve Hall said their farewells to the huge crowd of travelling fans.

Vila was always good to have on the team sheet, because he could put the fear of god into the opposition. His tactic of charging onto the ball and diving at opposing player's knees always guaranteed a quick play the ball, which gave the next man taking the ball up easy yards. But Vila could also be a liability – as I have just mentioned – because of his unorthodox tackling technique of which I copped a few stray ones. The other aspect was his level of fitness. If you didn't get him off at the right minute he would be giving penalties away because he could not get back onside. No matter how effective a player he was, a lot of teams played at him because he was not the most agile of players.

Shortly before the season ended I had signed a new three-year deal. It had been on the table a good while. There were no problems with signing it, more a case of when. I was playing some good rugby and other clubs were sniffing around me. But I got what I wanted, with everything geared up to me spending my last three years at Saints.

There had always been a touch of comedy around the contract situation during my time at Saints and I still laugh now at some of the things that had happened. On one occasion in the early 90s, Wigan had come in for me with an offer and Saints needed me to sign a new contract. I received a call telling me that I had to go round to director Tom Ellard's house. I was still plastering, so I nipped out of work for a couple of hours in all my dirty clobber.

When I got to Tom's house, all the rest of the board members were there and I wondered what the fuss was about. They made me a cup of tea and said, 'We would like to offer you a new deal'. They presented me with this new contract but I said, 'I don't want that, that is no good for me'. The next thing I knew was that Tom Ellard gave his wife a nod and she pulled another contract out of this briefcase.

This happened three times and Mrs Ellard just kept pulling them out of the bag.

When the last one came out I said, 'Before I sign are there are more in there?' But I still didn't sign anyway – I am not daft like that. I knew I was in a strong bargaining position.

Wigan came in for me five years running – they were always sniffing around. I reckon if it had not been for director Mally Kay I'd have probably ended up signing for Wigan. There was only Mally who could handle my sense of humour. Mally got a lot of flak after he left, but he worked tirelessly trying to keep the club from hitting the wall. If anybody slags him off to me, I say, 'You are not on, he is not that kind of bloke'.

The impact of the attacks on New York of September 11 reverberated around the game – and took its toll on the Australian tour to Great Britain. The Aussies, apparently, were fearful of having to fly over the Middle East during this turbulent time and initially the tour was scrapped. Eventually, they decided to come for a shortened tour – playing the three test matches and scrapping the games against the top five sides like Saints and Wigan.

Guinness were sponsoring this test series – and that might have played a part with me regaining my taste for international rugby. A few cases ended up coming the players' way during that series.

Some of the Aussie players, like Brad Fittler, didn't want to tour and there was a lot of speculation on whether they would come or not. In one sense it was easier for our lads to say, 'Why are these soft buggers not coming?' because we didn't have to fly the other way.

I was not bothered either way. On one hand the game needed a good Ashes test series to wipe out those miserable World Cup memories, but on the other hand if they didn't come it was going to be feet up time for a longer rest than I was used to.

Great Britain's preparation for the series involved a warm-up test against France in Agen. It was the first and only time I had skippered Great Britain, which was a real honour. I marked the occasion by scoring a couple of tries. I played left back row with Gary Connolly the left centre and we had some fun down that side. We butchered them really, which was pleasing. Although the French were full of enthusiasm it was over after 15 minutes. The second half became a case of everyone wanting to score and we drifted away from our game plan a bit.

It was a game that we needed and the preparation was good – going to Spain first for training, dropping in for the game in France and then back home for the First Test at Huddersfield.

The Great Britain squad had developed a new format in camp and although we still stayed at the Worsley Marriott, we were allowed to go home the day before each game and occasionally during the week. All the players were only an hour or so away from home so it made sense letting them nip back to their families.

GB had a new coach in Australian David Waite. There were a few sceptics, jumping on the bandwagon that an Aussie should not have been given the role. But I had a huge amount of respect for Waite – even if his sessions would go on too long some times. If he was speaking to you he would read your mind and say, 'I know I am running on, Joynty. I am going to finish soon'. Waite was good and improved even more when he began listening to the players.

If you take an overview, I reckon he has done a fantastic job and that is shown because every representative team is playing more regularly and against much better opposition. That is how you become a better rugby playing nation.

Rugby league needed a good series, particularly because there was a lot of the spin in the national press about it being a dying game. Stars like Jason Robinson, Henry Paul and Iestyn Harris had gone to rugby union and this was supposed to sound the death-knell for our game. We knew it was all rubbish, but we needed a good competitive series to avoid giving them even more ammo.

Unfortunately Great Britain had lost key players before the series – all three front line hookers were ruled out and we ended up playing experienced back rower Mike Forshaw there. At that level you need out and out sevens and nines playing and that was what we lacked.

Now Forshaw was one of the best tacklers in the business, but if you put his distribution next to Keiron Cunningham's, they are not on the same level. It was the same with Kevin Sinfield, a loose forward, who was slotted at scrum half.

It was just one of those things. How can expect to have a fully fit squad, firing on all cylinders at the end of a long hard season?

That said we still got off to a flying start at the McAlpine Stadium, with Scully working tirelessly and grabbing a brace of tries. After that I was quietly convinced we were going to win the series, even though I had been through this all before.

When we went to the review on the day after that game there was a real belief in the camp that we were going win the Ashes. We had been within touching distance back in 1994, but I was convinced we had an even better chance.

We had a good settled side that had been growing in maturity. Although I never officially became vice-captain to Andrew Farrell, I must have been there or thereabouts.

Sadly we never got a sniff in the Second Test, and the speccies were still filing into the Reebok when the Aussies scored their opener. When you are playing against quality opposition you have to start well and they stuffed us. It was 40–0 at one stage before we grabbed a couple of late ones to make it a little bit more respectable.

Despite that, there was still a feeling of confidence. It was not like my last couple of experiences with GB and I was loving it, and had recovered my appetite. The fact that former Wigan player Phil Clarke had come on board as team manager possibly helped that. That was a big plus for the lads because he knew what we wanted. There was a bit more innovation with team building. Instead of just going out for team meals, we all used to go out to watch film premieres together or to places like the Comedy Store.

There was a full house for the Third Test at Wigan and a magnificent atmosphere, but we lost. We made a solid enough start but it went away from us with half-backs Trent Barrett and Andrew Johns taking control in the final quarter.

I was gutted to lose that series – and kept thinking, 'I am running out of time here to do this'. An Ashes series win was one of the few things that eluded me in my career.

The last time Britain had won a series of any description, was against the Kiwis back in 1993. When the 2001 squad first assembled, there were only two people in that room who had been involved in a winning series – Gary Connolly and myself.

15

VOLUNTARY TACKLE?

So much for summer rugby! When we kicked our 2002 season off in the Challenge Cup against Oldham at Stalybridge football ground, it was freezing cold and just didn't stop raining all day. I was used to playing at Oldham's old ground, The Watersheddings, which was now long gone, but this was even worse with a really sloping pitch carved straight into the hillside. They had two fat props that day and I think they revelled in the conditions. They looked like twins after they had both been dipped in the mud, but give them their due they kept coming at us. Oldham treated it like their cup final and really tackled well.

In a bid to break them down Tommy Martyn tried to crack them open with a few sneak plays, desperate to use some of his flair to pull something out of the bag. But the conditions were just not suited to that and more often than not the slippery ball would hit the deck. I recall going over to him and saying, 'I don't think ploys like that are going to work today!' He knew what I meant and I think we just settled for grinding out a win.

I recall looking over to the dugouts where new Aussie signings, Darren Britt and Barry Ward, were sitting with blankets around them, probably wondering what they had let themselves in for.

We were all freezing and soaking wet and desperate to get into the warmth and get something hot inside us after the match. Unfortunately, somebody had tampered with the food that had been prepared for us. Thankfully the catering ladies, who were going to dish it up, noticed before they fed it to us. One of them said, 'I think somebody has been trying to poison you!' They ended up having to ship in 40 hot pies as a substitute!

The two Aussie props we had brought over were both good blokes, but in contrasting ability. When I first met the pair of them when they jetted in, they looked like a pair of hillbillies with their flip-flops and 1970s dress sense. But Britt was an outstanding forward who I had already played against. He got stuck in and gave a lot to the lads, particularly in terms of showing them how to get the ball out of the tackle. He was a fit fella, despite having the physique of a bush tucker man!

He took a lot of punishment when he hit the ball up, particularly late in his career. His wife and kids loved it in St Helens and they really took to it. Britty was great company to be with, he tells some good tales and was an all round good bloke. He had a very unorthodox running style and didn't lift his arms to fend, which meant he took a few high ones. I don't think he could lift his arms really, because he had both his elbows done in the past. He told me a tale about when he once had his knee and both elbows in plaster casts and his wife said it was like looking after an extra child 24/7.

I think Barry was fond of the delights of the Crispy Cod a bit too much mind. I was in the glass shop one day getting a pane of glass for my bookcase and Barry and his wife were in the chippy next door. He only told me this when he was leaving the club, but apparently his wife spotted me and said to him, 'Get your head down Barry, the captain is over there!' Both him and his wife were ducking down hiding all their food.

It was Tommy Martyn who introduced him to the Crispy Cod and I don't think Ian Millward was too chuffed with Tommy when he found out.

We went on a good winning run at the start of the year, but that ended when we got hammered at London on Easter Thursday. We had two games over Easter so coach Ian Millward decided to rotate the squad, soccer style, and perhaps the Easter Monday game against Wigan was given priority. I am not in favour of that tactic – it's one of those things you scratch your head over. Because I was not playing I didn't make the trip – it is a long way and they have to put you up in a hotel. It was a blessing because I heard it took a lot of our speccies eight hours to get down there, battling with the Bank Holiday traffic.

Four days later we beat Wigan at Knowsley Road in a tremendous game, which was closer than the 19–0 result suggests.

There were a couple of real match turning incidents, namely Tommy Martyn's instinctive blind pass that put Peter Shiels over for a try and Keiron Cunningham tracking back 50 metres to nail and turn Mark Smith at the corner when a game-breaking try for Wigan looked on the cards.

For that game, Sky did a head-to-head between Andy Farrell and me. It was my night, because I beat him hands down in all quarters; tackle count, metres made, breaks and offloads. Somebody said that if it had been the other way around they would have flagged it up more. It was flashed up Chris Joynt won the head-to-head, but there was no elaboration!

I have had some good tussles with Faz, because in that era particularly it was always my job to get a grip on him.

Our eyes once again switched to the Challenge Cup where we had to play Leeds in the semi-final, but we had one of those awkward fixtures playing the same opponents the week before. That sort of game was hard to play in because you are thinking about the following week, the only blessing was that it was at home.

It was significant for me in more ways than one. Leeds were in the lead at the hour mark and then I scored my first try of the season to bring us back in contention. They were still ahead in the last minute when I burst down the left and popped a round the corner pass out to Tony Stewart who waltzed in at the corner to clinch it for us.

My try was more significant though because it meant I could have my first drink for nearly four months. On 1 January 2002 I told myself I would not have a pint until I scored my first try of the season. At the time I assumed we would play some poor team in the opening rounds of the cup, where we would score 50 points and I could end my self-imposed drought. But well into April I was still tryless and beerless so when I charged onto the ball their new Aussie half-back, Ben Walker, seemed to just fall off me. He should have buried me but I think he must have known I wanted a drink.

That win gave us a bit of a psychological edge for the following week's semi-final, which was again at the JJB. It was one of those classic encounters – from a Saints perspective! Although both of our wingers, Darren Albert and Tony Stewart, grabbed hat-tricks that afternoon, it was our pack's display that really laid the platform. We blitzed them with a brilliant brand of football and I recall reading an article by Shaun Edwards in one of the papers in which he wrote that it was the finest display of rugby league he had seen, with the level of skill involved, offloading, passing and support play. If your team is getting praise from Shaun Edwards, you must be doing something right. We were on fire – and I am sure the millions watching it on *Sunday Grandstand* enjoyed it!

In the build-up to that game I had a call from a Yorkshire radio station, saying they wanted to interview me. I thought Leeds' coach Daryl Powell might have put him up to it. I am always a bit coy anyway, and said you can have an interview, but it might not be much use to you because I am doubtful with an ankle injury and not supposed to playing. The radio bloke said, 'OK, don't worry about it'.

Anyway on the game day itself I got into the lift at the JJB and Daryl Powell followed me in and he said, 'You are not supposed to be playing!' I knew exactly what he meant and suspected the interview was a put-up job. It might not have been – people talk and things slip out, but it is surprising how much opposing teams know about each other. Saints have had a few spies in the camp ahead of big games. The players talk, especially when you have good mates and brothers facing each other.

Some players were not as subtle in trying to winkle out information. Wigan prop Terry O'Connor used to be a dead give-away really because he would call me up and say, 'Nice day isn't it, Joynty'. The small talk like that would continue until it got to, 'How's your knee?' So I would think on my feet and never gave anything away. He must have thought I lived in cloud cuckoo land. It happened regularly but I don't know what he ever got from those conversations. Maybe he could get a job in MI5 with his strategy for extracting information!

Saints' stock was probably at its height after that semi-final game – but then it plummeted when we went to Bradford with a virtual A team and the ensuing mess dogged the build-up to the Challenge Cup Final.

Maybe it was stupid programming to have a semi-final on

Sunday, followed by a big televised Super League game five days later, only a week before the game's traditional showpiece final. It was a tough ask on the players ahead of the final – it was not possible to wrap all the players up in cotton wool and play them. Millward was concerned about preserving his team for the following week at Murrayfield.

We were meant to have 12 players injured – players always pick up knocks, but this was ludicrous. Apart from that I had always been in favour of hitting the ground running ahead of a big game. Unfortunately, I think we were all still in party mode after beating Leeds and getting through to the final. Missing out on that Bradford game simply gave us a week more to celebrate, which looking back is not the way you win cup finals. Mine and Newy's injuries for that game were so bad we had to go to York races that weekend and have a few pints by the river! There was a big furore and the club's medical team were tied up with trying to produce all the medical evidence to justify leaving us out.

It backfired in a way because all the build-up to the Cup Final was dominated by the talk about were we really injured and was it against the spirit of the game and cheating the paying public by fielding that side. Ironically, the issue would raise its head two years later, also at Bradford, with similar consequences.

There was an underlying fact that nobody wanted to talk about the Challenge Cup Final, one of the biggest events on the sporting calendar with over 100 years of history attached to it. You would get media questions like, 'Have you made a miraculous recovery?' It just kept stirring the pot.

All the spotlight was on Saints – as the big sinners, not as the team that had blitzed Leeds in the semi with that magnificent display of free-flowing football. Suddenly the neutrals were lined up against us and it soured our build-up and made every one in our camp a bit lacklustre. It was not a big laugh. This was serious stuff and we went up there on the back of a load of bad publicity.

It is an awkward one because from a player's point of view those of us who were not selected for the trip to Bradford were probably pleased, because it more or less guaranteed that we would be running out at Murrayfield in the final. On the other hand, we should have played to keep ticking over and keep our feet on the ground.

In the absence of a lot of first teamers, veteran prop Sonny Nickle ran his blood to water for 80 minutes and pulled his tripe out, but he did not even get the bench spot he deserved for the final. Sonny also missed out on a Grand Final spot later that season, which was a real shame because he should have been in the 17 on merit.

We tried to put all the fuss behind us when we headed north of the border that week. It started badly because although our hotel on the outskirts of Edinburgh was fabulous, the first thing we were told was every sports team that stayed there had lost. Most notably the England rugby union team had stopped there ahead of their Grand Slam bid that ended in failure. That was a bad omen. And the hotel was too big and like a rabbit warren. I was rooming with Newy again, but we never saw the other players apart from mealtimes and training sessions. It did not really work because the hotel was so huge you had to go and pack your flask and sandwiches to get to the snooker room and by the time you got there somebody else was already on the table.

The atmosphere in the build-up was not right and everybody was too relaxed. I am all for that but we took it too far. I also think Millward got a taste of his own medicine with regards to playing mind games with the media and the public. Wigan were supposed to have a load of players missing, all the rumours were rife about petty things, about trouble in the Wigan camp. It was all kidology.

It fooled some of their own speccies, because the Wigan public did not turn out, and they returned 5,000 tickets of their 13,000 allocation. I can remember when Wigan would take 35,000 to a big cup final! People in Wigan thought it was going to be a foregone conclusion. They would turn up and Saints would butcher them.

Although Wigan's players went into that game as underdogs, they had a lot more belief, and there was less pressure on them being the underdogs. Wigan played well but there were also a few points in the game that went against us. Keiron's disallowed try could have gone our way and a later penalty decision on their line went their way. Kris Radlinski came off his sick bed to play and win the Lance Todd, just as Ellery Hanley had done in 1991 with his hamstring. Rads was supposed to have a bad foot, and he probably did have a bit of an injury. If he had a bad foot, I wanted two of them. He had a tremendous game – he is a key member of their team and the inside info we had received was that he was not playing.

When the team sheets were read out, there he was.

We were duped as a whole and almost conned into believing that we were going to win; Wigan could not sell their tickets, numerous players were missing and we had just beaten them in the Super League.

They simply took their chances better and their big game players – Rads, Julian O'Neill, Adrian Lam and Andrew Farrell all clicked. I was absolutely gutted because this was the first time I had captained a side to defeat in a major domestic final and it was not a nice feeling. Paul Newlove had a good game that day and we voted him the players' player of the match, but on the whole we did not perform,

I had to give a speech at that evening's dinner and recall saying that we would come back better. The do at night is always sombre for a couple of hours, but we ended up having a good night and celebrating the achievement of getting to a major final rather than moping about the loss. It is not the same as winning mind, especially as some of our lads had probably spent their winning bonuses. I hadn't – I would sooner have it in the bank first!

The homecoming at Knowsley Road was an anti-climax because there had been so much expectation. We had not beaten Wigan in a Challenge Cup Final since 1966 and this was supposed to put it right. But we had a good time on the bus trip home and started drinking as soon as we hit the traffic on the M6. We sobered up so quickly when we got to the homecoming because it was such a contrast to previous years. There were only about a couple of thousand people there, where if we had won there would have been 15,000. That shows you the fine line between winning and losing in professional sport. Winners are grinners! Some of the lads who went on the microphone were a bit scathing of the speccies for not turning up, but I just saw that as an excuse on those lads' part. For the people who turned up, good on you. I have no axe to grind with those who did not – they were probably gutted too. It hit home to me that nobody wants to support losers!

It was a tough spell after the final and we threw away a 20-point lead at Castleford and lost. As skipper I used to look down the fixture list and see Leeds and Bradford coming up and think, 'Great' and get a real buzz. Then I would see Halifax and Wakefield and think, 'Oh no!' I was more wary of those games because I knew that my week as a captain, playing the so-called lesser teams, would be tougher. Standing in the dressing room at The Jungle or Belle Vue you can sense an atmosphere. It became one of the hardest parts of the job, lifting them for a game against sides, who would be treating games against us like a cup final. That had also been the case in years before – Cas, Wakefield and Sheffield were all bogey teams for this reason alone.

After that disappointment we went onto another good winning run – although that was temporarily interrupted with another of the game's harebrained schemes.

Midway through the season somebody decided that Great Britain should fly Down Under in the middle of our hectic league programme to play a one-off international. I am all for international rugby, but this was not like nipping over to France. It was a really dumb idea – and I don't think the players wanted to go. Saints had to play a tough game at Hull before jetting off, but some of our lads had to pack for Australia two days before that game. It was bonkers! We played Hull, won by a couple of points, were then ferried by minibus to the hotel and from there to the airport. It was a ludicrous idea and all the travelling was dreadful. We had no time to get jet-lagged because we were there and back in a week. It is the worst thing in the world to be travelling after taking a knock, especially when you are jetting 12,000 miles. The Aussies had just finished their Origin series and so they were all on song. No wonder Great Britain got slaughtered in what was our worst ever test defeat.

Frustratingly, it undid a lot of the good work we were patiently building up from after the fairly decent Ashes series the previous year. Things were looking on the up and all of a sudden they decided to play this game. It was the first and only time I played a Test match in Australia – but not an experience I enjoyed. I was pencilled in to start that day, but I was dropped down to the bench late in the day and replaced by Bradford's Stuart Fielden. I came off the bench but their new kid on the block, big Willie Mason, had already seen to it that there was not much left to play for.

Our squad stopped in the palatial surroundings of the Manly Pacific Hotel – it was a shame that the rugby spoiled that trip. While we were there, myself, Scully and kit man Stan Wall did the climb over the Sydney Harbour Bridge. You click onto the safety wire and away you go. That was a fantastic experience – I might put my name down for the Widnes-Runcorn Bridge crossing in future!

It was business as usual as soon as we returned to Britain and although we came unstuck at what was fast becoming our graveyard at the JJB, we soon put that behind us. And boy did we rattle up the points! In successive weeks we put 72 on Warrington, 34 on Wakefield, 50 on Bradford and 64 on Halifax. In three of those games we never conceded a try, which did wonders for our points difference.

The icing on the cake there was taking a full team to Valley Parade, where we had real fun. After a while Bradford were crying out for us to fetch the A team back on – the Bulls were badly wounded. Not only did we beat them on their own midden for the first time in Super League, we ran riot and stuck a half-century of points on them.

We were neck and neck in the league with Bradford, who had started the season by winning the World Club Challenge against Newcastle Knights. After the farce of the previous encounter we went there determined to do a job, and had picked out some weak spots. This was Lesley Vainikolo's first year. The Volcano was massive but we had done our homework on him and realised he wasn't so quick on the turn. He got singled out for special treatment from our kickers. Longy kept putting his kicks behind him and as quick as a flash Darren Albert would be in and hunting him down before he got going.

At this stage we were focused totally on finishing in the top spot, still we lost to Wigan again – this time 48–8. They seemed to have it over us and our run against them seemed to have gone.

We went down to London for the last game of the season and we had to win to finish in the sought-after top spot. It turned into a personal nightmare for me – even though we won the game.

I played no part in the London win after collapsing in the dressing room before the game and being taken to hospital. It seems it was a freak combination of things that caused it, starting with something as innocuous as me biting my cheek. When I took my gum shield out of my kitbag I noticed it was still a bit grubby from the week before so I cleaned it in mouthwash. I had also taken an anti-inflammatory tablet because I had suffered a knock the previous week. These were just little everyday things, but they reckon the mouthwash had gone directly into my bloodstream via the open wound in my mouth and combined with the anti-inflammatory tablet. I had got changed for the game when I started feeling myself going really itchy. Newy was sat at the side of me at the time and I turned to him and asked, 'Has my face gone red?' Shocked, he said, 'What the hell is up with you?' Newy was panicking that much he ended up sitting away from me so he was not part of it, if anything bad had happened to me. The next thing I just started dripping with sweat, then my throat started to hurt, which was the scary bit, and I collapsed. Dr Simon Perrett, the club doctor, actually saved me really by calming me down and sorting me out until the ambulance came.

It was not good for the rest of the lads preparing for the crucial game, so they got me out of the changing rooms and put me into the St John's Ambulance hut. I was sitting in the corner, half knocked out and all the St John's lot were huddled up saying, 'He looks bad!' I thought 'Cheer me up, why don't you'. Then one of them came over with a pen and programme and said, 'Mr Joynt, can I have your autograph please?' Although I did manage to scribble on it I was thinking wrong place wrong time son! When they said the ambulance was outside, I declared, 'I'm not going in my kit!' I have seen it before in the casualty waiting room where you see lads rolling up in their playing kit looking like bloody idiots. There was no way I was doing that. I suppose I was just being stubborn, but I made sure I got changed out of my kit.

Kel Coslett came with me in the ambulance and they had to give me a shot of adrenalin to bring me round. This young doctor came in to give me two injections and said, 'I haven't done this before. I need to get a senior doctor to supervise me'. I turned to Kel and said, 'No way is he doing it!' All I was thinking about was getting the bus home with the rest of the lads.

Although I saw umpteen specialists afterwards they could never pinpoint what the problem was. They said they could only do that if they took me in hospital for weeks on end and give me doses of the stuff in different measures to see how it affected me.

I had had a bad do earlier on in the season when I was with the Lancashire squad preparing for the Origin game against Yorkshire. I had been bad with the 'flu and lost a lot of fluids, so they put me on a saline drip. That not only replaced the fluids, but also acted as a relaxant. Well I was zonked, but unfortunately while I was out for the count, the fire alarms went off in the hotel. My room-mate John Stankevitch said, 'Joynty, wake up there's a fire!' Although I didn't know where I was I managed to get myself up and into reception where the firemen were running around all over the shop. It must have just been too much for me and I collapsed and banged my head on the floor, knocking myself out. I was only out for a short while, but when I came round a woman from the hotel was standing over me saying, 'Can you sign this disclaimer, Mr Joynt?' I just waved her away. It is probably a reflection of the claim-minded society we are living in today.

In the end we finished top of the league for only the second time in my career. That showed our outstanding consistency over the season. The following season they started awarding a League Leaders shield – something that was long overdue since they brought in the play-offs.

Our top place guaranteed us two bites of the cherry at home – we needed them because we came unstuck against Bradford in that opening game. They played the wet conditions better than us. All their tries that night came from kicks, particularly Paul Deacon's skidding grubbers. We came back really strongly – I was probably thinking about the time we had done them in 2000 and a lot of people in the crowd were anticipating that we were going to do it again. We left that game thinking, 'We'll have these Bulls in the final'. There were a couple of moments where we created chances at the back end, which just did not come off. Nobody was leaving the ground early. The other highlight was young Mike

Bennett going toe-to-toe with Lesley Vainikolo in the Restaurant End corner. Good on Benno for standing his ground! But if any of The Volcano's punches had connected, they would have been picking Benno's head up out of Piggy Fletcher's sty at the back of the ground.

We turned Wigan over in the final eliminator to book a return date with Bradford at Old Trafford. We all have different roles to play in the team and my job against Wigan was to marshal their extremely crafty scrum half Adriam Lam. The Papua New Guinea skipper had run rings round us on the previous couple of meetings.

My task, at loose forward, was to knock him on his arse every time he got the ball or went to kick it. He was absolutely sick of the sight of me. Admittedly sometimes I was about three seconds late, but it worked. The more I got to him, the easier it became because he would always have a sly look where I was and where I was going to hit him from. Any kicker under pressure is a bit wary, as Sean Long can testify with the blows he has taken over the years.

Somebody came up to me after the match and said, 'Do you not get on with that Lam or something?' But that is what I had been programmed to do that night. I really enjoyed playing loose forward that night because I was involved a lot more. The way the game had changed meant a second rower played more as a centre so you didn't get as many carries as you did a few years earlier. The game has moved on, but I always enjoyed playing at 13 and the involvement that came with it.

Beating Wigan is always special and that night was no different. About 4,500 fans were locked out. They missed a classic as we booked a place at Old Trafford.

In my reckoning, Bulls' week off, for beating us at the first hurdle, did them no favours. They were a huge side then and they needed a run out or a flogging to keep match fit. We went into that game having the upper hand because of that.

The final started badly as we lost full-back Paul Wellens in the opening minutes when he caught a boot to his face, smashing his eye-socket and cheekbone. We were a man down when Bulls shifted play right and with our defence stretched they scored in the corner. It was a good start for Bradford, who always came out of the blocks well. The opening exchanges were really fierce and everybody up in the stands expected Bulls to perform a demolition job on us, similar to what they had done to Wigan in the previous year's final. They were coming at us in numbers at the rucks, and we were just hanging on in there, soaking it up. We kept at them and held them out. After throwing all that at us we grabbed two tries to take a shock 12–8 lead at half time. Mike Bennett grabbed our first, mainly because Bradford stopped and looked at the ref instead of playing to the whistle. I don't think Benno could believe his eyes as the line opened up.

In the dressing room at half time my team talk was, 'They have thrown everything at us, but we are in front'.

Bradford tend to play well for the first 20 minutes and third 20 minutes. They really come at you, so the more you can keep them at bay the better. Bradford grabbed two quick tries after the break, but our game plan stayed the same because we knew they would tire.

It was a case of when and a lot easier said than done. Martin Gleeson slid over to level matters at 18-all to set up a gripping finale – and a drop goal competition!

In Paul Deacon they had an ace marksman, but we denied him a decent shot at the uprights. Our defence was desperate and we ran around like headless chickens to keep them out and applied plenty of pressure on the kicker.

Scully and Longy also had a few stabs at the drop goal before we finally hit the target. If you watch the build-up to that on tape, you can look on the negative side and think it could have been so different because their long ball down could have easily bobbled out of play after hitting Sean Hoppe which would have resulted in us dropping out.

On the positive side Choppy, Tony Stewart, Newy and Peter Shiels took the ball virtually the full length of the field playing open rugby to get us a target on goal. We were more switched on at that stage than Bradford, because we didn't stick it up our jumper to get to the last tackle kick. We showed a bit of flair, to get to 25 metres out. I got into the captain's mode and came up for the pressure drive on the fifth tackle, dived at their knees to get a quick play the ball to catch them on the back foot so Longy did not have as much pressure on him. Longy kicked it and the rest, as they say, is history. He has probably struck sweeter goals, but none as valuable as that.

Although there was barely no time left we knew these blokes have a good record of retrieving the ball from short kick offs, so the first call was, 'Let's just get it and secure it!'

I went from dummy half and was expecting to get creamed with one last hit, but a bit of smart play by Jamie Peacock and Paul Deacon saw how I was taking the ball in and pulled out of the tackle and I hit the deck. All of a sudden they sprung off complaining to the ref I dived and appealed for a penalty. But I know the rules and as long as I got up and carried on until their men tackled me I was OK. If I stayed on the floor like a dead fish it would have been a voluntary tackle. But I didn't, so all those pundits who were complaining about referee Russell Smith's failure to award a penalty afterwards were talking rubbish. There is no better sight in the world than seeing Jimmy Lowes jumping up and down because we have won again.

On my way to the press conference one of the women from Bradford asked, 'Did you dive then?'

To add a bit of spice I said, 'I did, yes!' because I didn't think it was a big deal.

'He did. He dived, the bastard!' she was shouting to all her friends.

I didn't know how serious it was then. The winners went into the press conference after the losers had been in and said their piece. Bradford had already stated their case about the alleged voluntary tackle, so when myself, Ian Millward and Sean Long went in that is all the media wanted to talk about.

I could not believe that these blokes could watch a gripping, thrilling and dramatic 80 minutes of football like that and then try and spin a line that it was somehow lost because of that incident. I have always believed in accentuating the positive – and there were plenty of good things in that game to write about.

The referees' controller Stuart Cummins agreed there was nothing wrong with what I had done, but at the end of the day we won the Grand Final by a single point. Pressure kick or not, if

Russell Smith had listened to the Bulls players and given in, Deacon would definitely have kicked it. But Smith ignored all the waving arms and shouts and screams, which meant we lifted the Super League trophy for the fourth time in seven years!

The season did not end there for me – I was back in camp with the Great Britain squad for the series against the Kiwis. That said, my mind was on other things – Andrea was pregnant and gave birth on Tuesday, 5 November, four days before the First Test. I was away in camp at the time, staying at the Worsley Marriott when I got a call at half past four in the morning. Andrea's sister was on the other end of the phone saying, 'Get yourself over here now!' I was rooming with Bradford's Jamie Peacock and when he heard me getting ready to go he said, 'Is it time?' And I just said, 'Yes, Joynty's life is about to change!'

It was hard, because under this new GB set-up we left camp and went home to our families the day before the game. Well, from purely a playing point of view, I could have done with staying at the hotel that Friday because that was the night the baby came home! So you can imagine there was not much sleep. Although I was getting carried away by the emotion of becoming a dad for the first time and my head was buzzing, on the other hand I had a Test Match to prepare for. Here we were, two new parents who still didn't know what we were doing, and I ended up getting no sleep the night before a big game.

It ended up being my last game for Great Britain. I'm not blaming the baby, but it might have been a wiser move to rest me in that game, and play me for the Second and Third Tests.

That opener was at Blackburn Rovers' Ewood Park, which was a bit away from rugby league heartlands and was another new ground for me. We didn't get much time on the pitch beforehand mind because of their over-protective manager. It was a good surface and stadium, but soccer people have this thing about letting rugby lads play on their pitches. Rovers' manager Graeme Souness didn't want us on the pitch to begin with, but we were allowed to train for 75 minutes on the turf.

Apparently Souness, in his best Scottish accent, had shouted, 'Get those bloody egg chasers off my pitch!'

When you think about it, we were a national team, preparing to take on the mighty Kiwis and we were getting turfed off ahead of the opening game.

It was a close game, but our winger Karl Pratt, had a shocker in spilling a lot of high cross kicks which resulted in tries for the Kiwis. I am not sure if he had had a baby too that week, but he hasn't played for GB since either.

The birth of baby Megan did not really hit home for me as a player then, because you are still caught up in the emotion of it all. I was also in camp, trying to get used to fatherhood and having no sleep. Whilst I was still in camp, Andrea's mum and dad were round for a couple of weeks so they didn't miss me – all the attention was on the baby. Any job is tough at that time and you struggle to come to terms with it at that level. Babies are the best things in the world, but they are also the most difficult things too. They don't do your rugby league career any good, but I had had a good innings because I was 30 then. There were players at Saints a lot younger than me – Scully, John Stankevitch and Keiron Cunningham – who all had kids and they dealt with it.

I had no specific preparations ahead of a match – and what routines I had went out of the window after our baby arrived.

The Second Test was drawn and we won the Third Test and I honestly believe that at that stage the players were giving the coach David Waite more respect with what he was trying to achieve. He stuck by that squad, and that, combined with Phil Clarke coming on board as team manager, Brian Noble as defence coach and Graham Steadman, we were getting our act together internationally after a very rocky patch.

16

GIVE US A PROP!

The bonus prize for winning Super League again meant that we had another crack at the World Club Challenge. This time the intensity of our preparation was not as good and we drew the short straw with our Challenge Cup draw the week before taking on the Sydney Roosters.

Our first game of the season was the cross-code game against Sale Sharks, which was not ideal preparation to get us up to speed for the Roosters. There seemed to be this infatuation with Wigan beating Bath all those years ago, and with Saints riding high, they decided to set this one up as a high-profile money-spinner. Maybe with ex-Saint Apollo Perelini playing for Sale and a few other connections, they might have thought it was a good idea.

Very few of our players had rugby union experience, and we had to bring in Gary French, who had been an England A international hooker, to give us a few lessons in the midweek prior to the game.

We ended up playing the union half first and to be honest I finished up running around like a headless chicken. When we got on the wrong end of one of those driving mauls I was thinking, 'This game is not for me!' We did not know what to do to stop them, because they just kept it tight and drove up the field like an eight-man solid unit.

Everything was about winning that night – some people criticised Sale for not playing a more expansive game and opening it up. They probably knew that if they gave us half a chance we would have taken it, so they kept it tight in the forwards and there was nothing we could do about it. We didn't know what to do, how to get hold of the ball and keep hold of it and ended up running around like a load of kids playing their first game of Bulldog. Even our own speccies were laughingly taunting us with cries of, 'You don't know what you are doing!' They were dead right.

Sale took a 41–0 lead at half time, but then we had to play catch-up in the second half.

We started off the league half well enough and I scored and Steve Maden went in and it seemed as though it was going to be a cakewalk. Then there was a 19-minute spell when we just couldn't score. Sale were well marshalled by Apollo and Jason Robinson, and they just scrambled well and kept us out. Because there was that much space, everyone was trying to score instead of playing rugby. By the time the penny dropped that we had to move the ball to find the gaps, it was a case of beat the clock. We rattled a few more in and just before the end we grabbed a try to peg it back to 41–39. Longy missed the conversion which would have tied it. If it had gone over everyone would have probably been shouting 'fix'.

I didn't have any regrets afterwards as a player, and probably came away with more respect for the Union code. I am sure, on the other hand, that there were a few non-players who were left with egg on their faces. It was a ludicrous plan really, played at completely the wrong time for us, when we should have been focusing on Sydney Roosters. To me it was all for the sake of a few quid – they got a 12,000 plus crowd, which they split so I hope it was worth it for them.

Our plans for the Roosters match went from bad to worse, with another spanner in the works coming in the shape of the cup draw. Anybody at home would have done, but we pulled out an away tie against the French team, UTC. It was the worst draw we could have had with what was facing us round the corner. They must have known how much I hated going to France. It was awful really, particularly as we flew from Stansted, which involved an horrendous journey to get there.

We could have done with a really competitive game – not a game against a team of muppets. Our forwards did really well that night and created a great platform for the victory and we ran in 70 points, but we needed a sterner test. After the game they flew us back to Manchester rather than Stansted, but the harm had been done.

We had a press conference to build up the World Club game and once again the British press corps seemed more fascinated by the Sydney boys; they seemed to be in awe of the Roosters. The tone of a lot of the pre-match coverage was again how many we were going to get beaten by.

The Roosters came better prepared than any other World Club side. The Aussies had lost the previous two encounters, against the Bulls and ourselves, which was embarrassing for them. They knew they had to come up with a performance to restore its credibility because some people had started saying, 'It is a tin pot pre-season trophy that the Aussies don't care about'.

Roosters played Widnes in a scrag game in the build-up to our match – and under new coach Ricky Stuart they were playing a very simple but effective game.

Our tactics were wrong in the game. We knew how dominant they were in the forwards, so our game plan was to try and get around the first three coming off the side of the ruck, and play around them. The Roosters soon clocked onto to that and we never really had any go forward.

Personally I think what we needed to do was meet fire with fire, but instead we were playing a style to keep us away from the full force of the hammer. We thought, 'Let's see if we can be smart and play a bit of football'. It didn't work because they just got off their line from the first whistle and really gave it to us. Everything we did, as a result, was off the back foot. Every time we gave it to Longy on the sixth tackle he was kicking it off our own 25 and they were running it back to us from their half way line. Their territory stats were unbelievable.

Looking back at the game, we had chances to score, but didn't take them. The Roosters were just a very patient team and they just plugged away and scored two just before the break. There was no comeback in the second half and we lost 38–0.

What hit home to me was that we had to start stepping it up a level. What they taught me was to do the basics in rugby league – and do them very effectively.

After that we had Bradford at home in our first Super League game of the season in a repeat of the Grand Final. They had all winter to simmer over that last gasp Old Trafford defeat. We knew how much they wanted to win – but no matter how that game went we would still have our winner's rings from the previous season.

For all Bradford's anger and frustration and the need in their eyes to right a wrong, we still kicked their arses that night. And we kicked them good style, which was even more pleasing. It was 24–6 at half time, grabbing four tries in a whirlwind 12-minute spell, and although they snatched a couple of tries from the restart, we were always in control and triumphed 46–22. It was not quite the script some people wanted to write.

We were embarrassed after our defeat against the Roosters and when you have a game as bad as that you need to get back onto the park.

We had to swap things around and although the team sheet had me down in the back row, with Jason Hooper at nine, I went to hooker that night and played around the ruck. Our forwards were tremendous, particularly Darren Britt, who had started the season tremendously well after playing the previous year with a niggling injury.

The intensity of the Roosters game did us good and we got off to a strong start to that season, going through to the Challenge Cup semi-final. We were playing a great brand of football, epitomised by a win over Castleford, which had everybody singing our praises. We gave them a 12-point start and then we just clicked and put 54 unanswered points on them in the last hour.

Everyone was building us up but in the run up to our semi-final with Leeds, the wheels come off at Huddersfield, where we suffered a shock 36–22 defeat. That was followed by a loss at home to Leeds, where former Saint Wayne McDonald went past me and ran almost the full length to score the winner.

I could sense there was something wrong, but could not put my finger on it. After winning our previous two semi-finals against Leeds at Wigan, the Rhinos were keen to make sure they got this game on their side of the Pennines this time and this one was played at Huddersfield.

The game could have gone either way, but it just did not happen for us. We had clawed our way back from 18–6 down and when centre Darren Smith went over three minutes from the end, it looked as though we had snatched the win. We had played some good football too, but lady luck was on somebody else's side that afternoon and that is basically what it came down to.

We were short on front rowers so I had been propping that afternoon, but was off the park in the closing stages. It was terribly frustrating to watch young Danny McGuire go over in the dying minutes. When Kevin Sinfield kept his head to boot over the conversion from the touchline, straight away I thought, 'They have the luck on their side today'. I am not knocking Kevin's kicking – just referring to the intense pressure he must have been under with that conversion. That kick forced 20 minutes extra time and I did not play in either of those periods.

As club captain, it was bitterly disappointing to be left kicking my heels on the bench at such a critical time. There may not have been room left with interchanges, but I strongly believe that the captain must be there with his team when it comes to that kind of conflict. Sitting on the bench at the time all I could think was, 'I should be on this pitch now! There must be some reason why I am not'.

Unlike Saints, Leeds took their first chance of dropping a goal and from then on we were up against the clock. They played it quite smart and then hit us with another late try.

We needed a win that afternoon to kick our season on, but that defeat knocked us down badly. It was so draining, it took so much out of us and it was probably the first sign that we were not going to regain our Super League title that year. It took away a lot of confidence and the feeling of invincibility we had. They had done to us what we had been used to doing to other teams. It was because we had got to the final hurdle and just clipped it with our trailing leg that made it worse. It was a really damaging defeat.

It was the first time we had lost a semi-final since 1994, which had also been against Leeds, and that made it three defeats in a row for us. That was unheard of because Saints were not used to losing three games on the spin. But it got worse – we went to Wigan on Good Friday and lost again to a side missing nine first teamers and fielding a load of young lads. Even Maurice Lindsay had been going around before the game giving his excuses as to why they were going to lose. We got off to a flying start, leading

22–12 at half time, but failed to score in the second half. They just stuck to their guns and consigned us to four defeats in a row.

All of a sudden the newspapers were talking about how much money we had missed out on by not going to Cardiff and then we started getting all the rumours about players being sold on. As captain you are left up to pick up the pieces and are the first port of call for unsettled team-mates asking what is going on. Eight players were ear-marked to go out on loan and although none of them actually ended up going, it did create a bit of unrest in the camp.

The salary cap also became an issue because we ended up having two points docked for alleged breaches in 2002. It was something to do with the way our bonuses had been paid and had we been paid differently, the club would have been within the rules of the cap. The club was never in a financial crisis – it was a case of making adjustments to fall in with salary cap regulations. Chairman Eamonn McManus and chief executive Sean McGuire came up with different formats for paying us our winning bonuses and that resolved the issue.

The club was also rocked by the news that one of our backroom staff, nutritionist Mike Sutherland, was not adequately qualified to do the job and he had to leave. The revelations and explanations behind Keiron Cunningham's failed drug test also came out around this time.

There were also a lot of rumours and gossip-mongers, so much so that the club's official message board had to be taken down. It became a case of make a story up and then somebody else would add a few lines and pass it on. You don't hear rumours when things are going well – that underlines the importance of winning and carrying on winning.

That year there constantly seemed to be something to take us off the scent of what we were supposed to be doing, which was winning matches.

There were some real lows – getting turned over by Wakefield at home and being booed off. You have to take stuff like that on the chin. There were just no excuses, even though many were offered every time we lost. I think those explanations that were offered shied away from confronting the core of the problem. We had gone into the season short of a prop forward and I had ended filling the role a few times, which showed how desperate we were.

I was not the answer in the front row, but we were running out of options. Veteran Sonny Nickle had been let go and Peter Shiels, who could play prop, had also left in the close season to be replaced by another back rower. Although Darren Britt was outstanding that year, Barry Ward could only play about nine minutes each half. Mark Edmondson was still developing in that position, so Millward ended up trying to throw young lads like John Stankevitch, Stuart Jones, Mike Bennett and Timmy Jonkers up into the engine room. It was not that those lads were not up for it, they just were not seasoned in that role. Things take time, especially at prop. And because those lads were athletic, Millward thought they could play there and soak up the punishment for daft minutes, and kept them on too long.

We went to Hull that season and Millward told me, 'I am putting you on the bench and I want you to replace Barry Ward after 20 minutes'. Well I had just got comfortable on the bench and just after nine minutes I was on! Most good teams had four good props, rotated every 20 minutes, but we were playing on two.

There had been a lot of talk before they brought in this new interchange system, saying it would benefit the teams who could rotate their big men. Talk became very cheap because we were ill-equipped to deal with the changes. I take a leaf out of Bradford's book, because after 20 minutes you would see Paul Anderson and Stuart Fielden trot off, but then you immediately get two other big lumps coming at you as fresh as daisies. I am not saying they were as good as our Saints lads, but they could do a job for a short time. We had nobody there to soak it up and dish it out. We had no foundation to build on.

Personally, I think the white flag had come out. This was probably the worst season I could have picked for my testimonial year – the timing was horrendous because things just did not happen for us on the pitch as a team.

I really enjoyed my testimonial and had some fantastic times and met some great people. Being a Wigan lad it was good because I was able to get out and about among the people in St Helens and

I had no problems with banter with fans, as long as I had given 100 per cent on the park. That is what I pride myself on, but as captain I was getting it from all angles.

My testimonial committee did a great job as a whole and my treasurer, chairman and secretary – Barry Hyland, Aidan Shukie and Gary Edgerton – all did a cracking job and worked really hard. There were events every month and the good nature of the town meant clubs and pubs were putting different things on. We had some good nights and trips which have given me plenty of memories.

Some thought they had done away with testimonials, because we are all earning better money now. But if you compare us with say Ryan Giggs, who had a testimonial at Manchester United, we are miles apart compared with the money the soccer players are getting.

Towards the end our season picked up a bit, with the highlight being a tremendous 35–0 win at Odsal – our first there since the advent of Super League. I scored that night, on a night that threw it down with rain. Our pack was great and it was just brilliant to lay one of those ghosts to rest. It meant that Odsal was no longer a bogey ground for us.

I played that night with a badly broken nose picked up at Headingley, but there is nothing you can do to protect an injury like that. A few of their players must have been short of violin practice because every time they got hold of me they rubbed their forearms across my face! Andrea was not best pleased when she first saw the state of it! Usually if you get your nose broken it gets knocked back into shape the following week, but that one was a bad 'un.

I was relatively lucky with injuries during my career. I never lost a tooth, although I had plenty chipped. I could not wear a standard gum shield because it made me sick. One time I came off and put my gum shield in a subs jacket and forgot about it. I thought I had lost it. I was gutted so I got a new one, which was never the same. Six months later I came off and put a subs jacket on and my gum shield was there. It was like finding a gold bar – I was made up!

For a large part of that season I had been playing with a knee cartilage injury that needed cleaning up, but I could never find a gap in the year. It needed sorting out, because I was struggling because of the swelling that flared up after training. It got to the point where I was doing more rehab than training. Wear and tear in my knee has been an occupational hazard and this was the sixth time in my career I had it done There is not much left of the cartilage now, it just gets trimmed, cleaned and shaped each time. You actually get the operation videoed now.

There was a bit of pressure on me to come back earlier, because Scully was also out injured. So I started training on it when it was not quite right, and that set me back a bit more.

Sean Long took the captaincy in my absence and kept the armband for the final two games on my return. I have no qualms with Longy or Millward for that matter, but maybe the coach could have spoken to me about it a bit more that week. I had been off for nine matches, so didn't expect to walk back in as captain. I needed to command the lads' respect again and could only do that by playing. But on the other hand I could sense that this was the time to give up the captaincy.

Our last game of the season was the play-off knockout against Wigan at the JJB. Again I started off from the bench. To play in so many games from the start and then all of a sudden you start to come off the bench was tough. It might be tactical, but I am still a firm believer of picking your best 13. My times on the bench were usually because I had not made the starting line up rather than being a tactical substitution.

I was glad to see the end of that year.

There were a few departures that season, including Tommy Martyn, who went to Leigh in August. He did not really want to leave Saints, but he got this opportunity to go to his home town club and help guide them to Super League. It was sad to see him go because it was another one of the gang gone.

About this time Saints also announced that they were signing Wille Talau and that more or less marked the end of Paul Newlove's hopes of getting a new deal at the club. By the end of the year Tommy, Newy, Darren Britt, Darren Smith and Wardy had all gone. We had all knocked about together because we were the same age so it was a bit of a depressing time.

My mate Dave Lyon, who had done a good job with the academy, also had to move on because they made the post full-time and he was unwilling to give up his good job at Wigan council. Dave is exactly the same as me in the sense that he calls a spade a spade. Dave could do a job and was up front and outspoken in what he wanted. He did not mind voicing his opinion and that is how it should be. There is not enough of it in rugby league.

So that was a lot of the old heads gone – apart from me!

Millward had a bit of an age obsession – anybody over 30 was 'past it'. He would be in team meetings saying, 'The average age of this team is 23, but Joynty over there is 32'.

Towards the end of that season, national papers began running stories that I had signed for Leigh. I don't know who had started those stories. It had been a tough year and I ended up having a home truths meeting with Ian Millward. We had to fill in a sheet saying what had gone right and wrong that season and were told to fill it in honestly. He was going home to Australia and summoned me to a one-to-one meeting. If I had not been so strong-headed he would have got shot of me then. He more or less said, 'It is time you were on your way because things haven't worked out'.

All the emphasis seemed to be on me and that is why I shifted some back onto him. We ended walking out of there with me saying, 'I am going nowhere, I'll see you next season!' There was no way I was going anywhere.

I had no problems once I had been up and said my piece, but I knew the team and thought he was getting at the wrong people. My testimonial was used to point out my performance from that year, and maybe it does have an impact in certain aspects. But on the other hand I thought I handled it pretty well and I am the sort of bloke who enjoys being busy. The testimonial had never stepped in the way of my rugby commitments – I would never go out the night before a match for example.

My frustrations probably came out then, because I had been at the club all those years and was still trying to get the date to play my testimonial game. I had everything in writing, which was legally binding, stating they had to give me a game, but I could never get a decision on when it would be. If they had told me straightaway I would have been happy. In the end they arranged a game for the following year.

In retrospect maybe we should have had that home truths meeting after the Leeds semi-final defeat? That would have probably cleared a few more festering things up and the season could have been a lot better. When I told Millward what I thought was wrong, I was telling him for his own good, not for mine. I don't regret doing it, but he was probably not used to being told.

We had the Aussies over again, but although I was not selected, I still had a phone call from Great Britain coach David Waite who said, 'You are not in my plans so I don't want to keep you hanging around a hotel in camp. But keep yourself fit and I will give you a call if I need you'.

There was also talk about playing for Ireland in the European Nations Cup, I only considered it to wind Basil up plus I was probably thinking of a few weeks drinking in Dublin.

More than anything I was just keen on having my first proper off-season since the early 90s when I was part-time.

17

THE LAST WALTZ

As I approached the 2004 season, I always knew it was likely to be my final year as a player. Pre-season training started in November, which was unheard of for me as usually I was still in camp with the Great Britain Test squad.

Saints had brought Apollo Perelini back into the fold as fitness coach and conditioner and it was definitely a case of things going full circle on the training routines. His pre-season work-outs took us back to the mid 90s when Wiganer Jack Penman was our weights trainer.

When Apollo returned, he basically opened up Jack's old book and adopted all the conditioning stuff we had done with Shaun McRae. Apollo also added the things that he had picked up along the way in his job in rugby union.

As a squad we also started wrestling over at Roy Wood's place, the Aspull Olympic Wrestling Club in Wigan. Roy was well respected in his field and had wrestled over the world – not the stuff on TV but freestyle competition wrestling. His role was important, because it had been identified that the floor area had been a weak spot for Saints in the previous season. We were not winning the ground after the tackle, which was punishing us.

It was the best off-season we'd had in a very long time and we had a decent foundation to build on. We played a couple of friendlies, the first against Salford and then against Widnes for my testimonial. There was a lot of fuss about my benefit match with people reminiscing about my career and talking as if I had already packed up! That game was just what I needed to kick up for the season ahead. I meant business, I was fit, didn't need any surgery and just wanted to get a lot of the previous season's frustration out of my system. The goal I set myself was to play in every game, because Millward had more or less told me in our meeting at the end of the previous year that I did not figure in his plans for 2004.

When he told me that, I don't think he could believe my response: 'This is music to my ears. I need a challenge in front of me at this stage of my career!'

I was up against a group of up and coming back rowers. As long as everyone is on a level playing field and there is no preferential treatment then it is good to have healthy competition.

We had bags of competition for places with Jon Wilkin, Timmy Jonkers, John Stankevitch, Lee Gilmour and Mike Bennett battling for a spot in the second row, although a couple of those lads were still injured from the previous year. But in that pre-season I made sure I trained harder than ever.

They had brought in Gilmour from Bradford to play left hand sided second row. I had already been shifted from that spot a couple of years previously, playing loose forward and right hand sided second row. Saints' defensive patterns meant that the right sided second rower defends like another prop. At about this time I started thinking that I could take up a new career in American Football, being brought on simply for defensive stints! Admittedly I had lost a yard of pace, but still had my worth within the team. My role was to carry the ball forward and just tackle like mad. My average tackle count was around 25 per match, sometimes going up to 35 depending on how many minutes I was out there.

We started the year well enough, winning our Super League opener against Hull, which was just what we needed, especially as they had brought over a few major new signings. The following week we played Bradford away in the cup. The Bulls had just won the World Club Challenge so all the talk in the press was about them. But when you have been up there at the top, you can stay on a roll or you can come back down to earth.

We did a complete job on them, which set the tone for the opening half of our season. The rugby we played that afternoon at Odsal was foolproof. There was nothing fancy about it, just a case of doing the basics really well. They had no answer to us around the ruck. With all the wrestling we had been doing, nobody could lick us on the floor. We were so quick in that area that it was unbelievable.

Now Saints have never really had much luck in the Challenge Cup draw wise – and I could have predicted we would pick another big team in the next round. League leaders Leeds came out of the hat with us, but at least we were at home.

When people ask me, 'Who do want, Joynty?' I always say, 'Anybody at home!' That is all you want in the cup, because you have to beat the best to win it.

Our tackling display against Leeds was superb and we were working a new defensive pattern. We were going out wider, so our tacklers were hitting the Leeds players from the outside. This was harder for the ball carriers because they could not see us coming. They had a few lads, like prolific scorer Danny McGuire, whose evasive style is all about avoiding tackles so he probably didn't relish the physical contact side of the game.

That afternoon I did my first ever suplex, which is a wrestling move where you grab your opponent from behind and throw them over your head. I 'suplexed' their Aussie half-back Andrew Dunemann. Although I don't think that throw was meant to be used on a rugby field, I thought I would give it a go. Leeds coughed up a bit of ball that day under the ferocity of our tackling.

It was a good win, especially as there had been a lot of talk in the press about what Leeds were going to do to us.

The draw again did us no favours – although Whitehaven and York were still left in the hat, this time we pulled out Hull.

Looking back, the Challenge Cup quarter-final against Hull was the hardest game of the whole competition, and I am counting the final in that. That game was so intense and in the balance until the final hooter, it could have gone either way.

Hull took a 12–0 lead but we stuck to our guns and kept at them. Again our defence was awesome, because we were defending a lot more rigorously and doing the basics well. That meant we were getting our chance with the ball, holding it well and getting a good kick in.

Teams were coming and throwing everything at us, but we were the fittest we had ever been due to the wrestling and Apollo's work. Everyone was injury free, although Mike Bennett suffered a bad leg injury in that Bradford game. When Benno got injured I thought, 'Millward must be eating humble pie now because he needs me more than ever.' One minute he said I didn't figure in his plans, next thing John Stankevitch and Timmy Jonkers were being joined by Benno on the sidelines. So I was an integral part of that team. Had I been less positive in that earlier meeting, maybe we would not have been in a position to go through to the next round of the cup! Personally I was more determined than ever, because I wanted to finish as a winner because that is what people associated me with during my time at the club.

Our season was going spectacularly well and then we got to our Good Friday game with Wigan which had the lot – big crowd, a punch up and a last gasp Sean Long drop goal to snatch a 21-all draw. The intensity and speed of such games are like playing at Test level because things happen so much quicker. Your reaction time is shorter and you have no time to blink. Our kicking game was exceptional, Sean Long was on fire, but our pack was laying him a good platform.

That Wigan game was followed three days later by the controversial Bradford away match on Easter Monday. If you look back over my career – and the 90 years preceding it – apart from a few exceptions, there have always been two games over the Easter period. It is a massive ask on the players, but it is the same for everybody else. It just seems like it is always Saints who are moaning about it. Really you just have to turn it into a positive, cut the talk about it not being fair on the players, send your strongest team and play the game.

I was one of only a handful of regular first team players who played at Odsal that day. Although I had been aware of the talk over Millward resting players and others carrying injuries, when I joined the team at Birch Services that morning I thought I had got on the wrong coach. I recognised very few of the lads who had already boarded at the club.

For away games I always met the team coach at Birch Services to save myself an extra two hours of travelling to St Helens and back out. It also meant that when I returned I could always get last orders at my locals in Wigan – the Brocket and the Cherry Garden.

Although we gave a good account of ourselves at Odsal, it was still kind of embarrassing to be playing for Saints alongside lads whose names I did not know.

Millward asked me if I would be captain that day and I obliged because I knew what those young kids were looking for was a calming influence so they could say, 'At least Joynty is out here with us!' That is what they needed because it was like throwing the Christians to the lions!

In my team talk before the game I told the lads, 'If you never get a chance to wear this jersey again, at least you are wearing it now and it is something you can say you have done. There are thousands of people out there who would love to say that.' I knew they would give it their best shot.

We actually took the lead in that game when Martin Gleeson went over for a try. But we lost Jon Wilkin, who was sent off early on for a high tackle on their scrum half Paul Deacon. It then just became really one-sided.

The decision to field a weak side came back to haunt us. I am all for squad rotation, but at the end of the day you have to put your best team on the park. You can get away with resting one or two players, but don't take the piss and say they are all out injured. There are always going to be injuries during busy spells but if a lad is playing well, let him carry on playing. If he is close to burn out, rest him then but don't do it with the whole team at the same time!

The next thing I knew about anything was going down to the newsagents and seeing a picture of Sean Long opening his front door plastered across the back page of the *Daily Mail*. I thought to myself, 'Rugby league doesn't usually get back page treatment!'

It later turned out that Long and Martin Gleeson had backed against Saints, predicting Bradford would win that game by more than nine points. But they both got caught out – and that was bad news for the club.

I think Saints as a whole were in the firing line really – not Longy and Gleeson – because we'd had this problem at Bradford back in 2002 when there had been a big fuss about team selection. Back then there had been a big tribunal. Once again Saints had upset a lot of people again with what had happened with our weakened team – and the implications this time were terrible.

With regards to what Longy and Glees did, the word stupidity springs to mind. It was hard to have sympathy for them because they are smart enough lads to think about what they were doing. Afterwards, when it hit home, I don't doubt they sat back and thought, 'What the hell have we done?' And if you speak to Longy now he will hold his hands up and say, 'I was stupid!'

But all the fuel had been added to the fire because we had again sent a weakened team to Odsal. The fact that it became diverted into focusing purely on the gambling issue probably took the heat off the coach's decision to pick an under strength team in the first place.

The press coverage once again proved we are a minority sport, even though we all think it is the best in the world. The only way we could command any back page headlines was with a knocking story. It was another excuse to knock our sport and who better to have a pop at than the most successful team in Super League and particularly Longy, one of the best players in world rugby. Longy took the brunt of the flak, but Gleese took a month's heavier ban because he had actually played and scored in the game.

But before they were punished, an investigation was carried out which meant they could continue playing. They were both playing magnificently too, but there was a cloud over us.

However, the lads dealt with the situation with a large dose of black humour. You would get into the dressing room and hanging off the wall there would be a defaced poster of Longy, with the words 'Wanted dead or alive!' scrawled across it.

We played Huddersfield in the Challenge Cup semi-finals, who seemed to fancy their chances going into the game. Giants were coached by Saints' former assistant Jon Sharp, and there was all this talk that he knew all our players' attributes inside out. That probably worked in our favour really because he was going down our teamsheet, not just the star men, which must have then been overload for their players. In times like that you can focus too much on the opposition rather than your own team. The rest is history; we kicked ass that afternoon and battered them.

The saddest part of that day was young hooker Mickey Higham turning his ankle during the pre-match warm up. It was a baking hot day and I kept thinking, 'Where's Mickey?' because we were expecting to see him come on and help us out. None of us realised at the time he had broken his ankle. He was devastated to miss out on the final because he was playing so well.

We were full of enthusiasm for the final at Cardiff – it was my first time at the Millennium Stadium and the fact that we were playing Wigan made it extra special.

I am not saying the word revenge was predominant, but in St Helens there was a lot of talk about 1966 because that was the last time we had beaten Wigan in a Challenge Cup Final. We were also really sore from losing at Murrayfield two years previously and desperate to make amends.

It was probably my last chance of playing in a Challenge Cup Final so I was really chilled and excited at completing one of the goals I had set at the start of the season.

The Cardiff experience was very enjoyable and everything went according to plan. Everyone was relaxed and we stopped off at Stoke City for our dinner on the way down.

Of course I had been used to rooming with Newy, but he had gone, so they put me in with newcomer Nick Fozzard. Although Nick seems to have been around for ages, this was his first major final and he was a nervous wreck. He had won nothing previously in his career and you could sense that nervous excitement coming off him. He was like my little girl in asking questions all the time. 'What is this for?' and 'What happens when the final whistle goes?' He kept waking me up and it was like a giddy five-year-old kid waiting for Father Christmas but in a 26-year-old's body.

We got off to a cracking start with an early try from Lee Gilmour and won the match 32-16. Despite the scoreline it was a really evenly matched game. We wanted it more than Wigan and that showed in the little things that we did better than them, such as the pressure we put on the kickers. Everybody contributed in their own little way and Wello scored a really crucial try just before the break. I just think our desire saw us through.

I had quite a duel with Andy Farrell and they put me there to do a job on him. Playing down that side was a blessing because at least I had the shade of the stadium roof. I don't relish playing in the heat and it was intensely hot that afternoon.

We have played Wigan a number of times where we have lost

leads, but we had enough steel in there. That was put into us because we had beaten all the other top six sides on the way to the final. We were thinking, 'We have come this far there is no way these swines are having this.' That was the mentality through the week and that saw us through a sticky patch in the game when Wigan looked like mounting a comeback.

It was great stadium to play in and the crowd was really right on top of you.

On a personal note, it was the first time my daughter Megan had been taken to the game and Andrea, her mum and dad and my mum and dad all went. They brought Megan down to the dressing room afterwards, although I couldn't take her onto the pitch. We were told if we took our kids onto the playing area we would be fined £15,000. They had the same rule in place the following week when Millwall played Man United in the FA Cup Final. A few of the soccer lads might have taken their kids on, but their bonuses were bigger than ours to pay out the fine!

The lap of honour was magnificent, and I remember Jon Wilkin getting to grips with this blow up Spiderman with a Saints shirt on. That thing followed us around and even turned up at the homecoming. Afterwards in the dressing room the celebrations began and we bumped into former Saints centre Scott Gibbs who came in to see us.

The only downer on the Cardiff experience was the two teams were placed in separate rooms afterwards so we could not mix with each other. It went against the traditions of rugby where you could knock seven bells out of each other on the pitch and then go for a few pints afterwards. I wanted to bump into my mates Faz, Gary Connolly and Terry O'Connor after the game, especially because we had won. My best pal Dave Lyon, who was the Wigan academy coach then, was also there with his wife and I wanted a drink with them as well.

After leaving the ground the team split up and we ended up going back to the Angel Hotel on the corner. Unfortunately every man and his dog was in there too.

It was good walking back to our hotel because fans from across the country were coming up and having their pictures taken with us. I imagined Ryan Giggs walking back like this the following week after the FA Cup Final.

We butchered Warrington the week after the Cardiff final and we believed we were invincible, more so when we carried on winning against Bradford. But then we started showing the first signs that the wheels were about to come off. We were hammered by Wigan at the JJB, but the flaws had been creeping in prior to that on the field and in training. We were no longer doing the little things like stopping out training for an extra 10 minutes. We had to be prompted to do a bit extra. Even in the gym all of a sudden there was a lot more chatter and people talking about 'how good the wedding was' and enjoying the honeymoon!

If you looked at the first half of season everyone was out early for training, but now they were just reminiscing. Perhaps it was a case that we had a lot of lads who had never won a Challenge Cup before and this gave them new found stardom in the town. But winning the cup doesn't give you the right to do what you want.

Instead of using the Cardiff success to kick us on to do the double, we seemed to settle into bad habits. We needed a kick up the arse because the honeymoon period took some getting out of, and some never did. This was not like 2001 when our squad was decimated by injuries after winning the treble, this time the squad was still healthy. Maybe players were looking for excuses – I know the fans wanted a win and were thinking, 'This is not the same team!'

We got a real thumping at Wakefield and I came off injured with my shoulder. My neck was already hurt before the game and when I went for my dinner beforehand with my mate Winny. He said, 'You can't play tonight, Joynty. Look at the state of you!'

I was on anti-inflammatory tablets and told Millward I was not 100 per cent fit with my neck. I ended up playing about 16 minutes, but after making a couple of tackles I came off holding myself so awkwardly that everybody thought I broken my arm. It was just a trapped nerve, but it kept me out for a month. Scully was also out, Longy had been suspended for three months and the team was lacking leadership.

Longy was badly missed because there was nobody who could step up immediately at scrum half. Wello filled in for a bit and then young James Roby performed well there later on. It showed, because although we only had a couple of injuries and absentees, we fell apart. We had no kicker – the game these days is about territory and we were never in good positions because we had nobody who could kick a ball like Longy. We were also lacking the little general and were not adhering to game plans.

My first game back after injury was at Salford on a roasting hot day and I played long minutes. Although Salford were scrapping for their Super League survival, they hadn't the sort of personnel we had. And even though we had a couple of lads missing, we should not lose at places like that. That defeat meant there was no way we could finish in the top two of Super League, which was our team goal at the start of the season.

It got worse and I was sitting in the dug out for the Leeds game when they put 70 points past us. I was speechless – it was unbelievable. Leeds were rampant and they butchered us. We just had no answers.

Our record at the back end of the season was shocking. After May, we did not beat another top six side and lost nine out of our last 14 games. I had been at Saints long enough to see coaches depart with a better record than that. But I guess the board must have faith in Millward.

We finished the season with a bit of a flourish and when we went to Warrington and won, the wheels seemed to be coming back on. Everything had been upped in training in anticipation of the play-offs, but I thought it was too late. We even went back wrestling which had been stopped after Cardiff.

Going into a game is not like a light switch, you can't just turn it off and on. It was too late when we tried to pick it back up again because we had already flat-lined so to speak. It took a while to crank it back up – and time is what we did not have.

It was very disappointing to lose that opening play-off game at Wigan. In the dressing room afterwards I was sat there thinking I don't want to finish here. We should have had it won by half time but we did not have the killer punch that we had in previous years.

Although I knew it could have been my last game as we walked over and clapped the Saints fans, I did not want it to be. Throughout my story I talk about losing to Wigan – but that night as I was walking off I was thinking to myself, 'I am going to have to live with the thoughts of losing my last ever game to these bastards for the rest of my life!'

On a personal note it was probably one of my best performances of the year, even though we did not win. A lot of the lads had been asking what my plans were, because they were aware it was my last match but I kept saying 'I don't know, I have to think about it!'

18

HANGING UP MY BOOTS

It was tough to finally make that decision to hang up my boots but I wanted to make sure I got it right. Everything had been geared up to finish at the end of the 2004 season. If I had said I was finishing immediately after my last game and then another offer, too good to turn down had come in, I would have looked daft. I could not rush this one.

There were plenty of offers from other clubs and I weighed them all up, but in the end I decided I was never going to play for another club after Saints.

Not being one to rush into anything, I took 10 weeks before officially announcing my retirement. During that time I was up and down. Some days I would wake up and think, 'I fancy carrying on!' Although I am in good nick, anything could have happened in another year. Paul Newlove is a good mate of mine and talking to him, one of his biggest regrets was not retiring at Saints, instead he went on for another year at Castleford. I did not want to make that mistake. Dave Lyon is another lad whose brains I picked and talking to him helped me.

The deliberation did have its funny side. Andrea was probably sick of the sight of me early on and some days she would see me in the house, where I would normally be out training and say, 'For God's sake play another year!' I think she was wondering if I really was ready to retire, but she has always let me sort my own career out and has played a supporting role in the background.

One of the things that swayed my decision to call it a day was the fact that over the last 18 months I had no longer been scoring the tries that I used to, even though I had my own part within the team.

The game today is about pace and it became really frustrating during points of my last season when I would see gaps, go for them and then just get ankle tapped. That happened a few times in the league game at Warrington.

Perhaps a lot of my memories and achievements will only sink in after I have spent a few more months on the sidelines, but I could not have done any of that without the help of a fantastic group of team-mates. I have played in some outstanding teams and we recorded some fantastic achievements. I will also miss running out of the tunnel with a packed Popular Side in front of me.

In the week I announced my retirement, the hardest part was watching the lads turn out for pre-season training in their snazzy new training tops. Again I started thinking, 'Shall I have another year?' But then again after winning the Challenge Cup in 2004, at least I know I am going out at the top.

I have thoroughly enjoyed my playing career – rugby league has been good for me and even though I have stopped playing I will still be taking a keen interest in the game.

Rugby league is constantly evolving - I should know it has changed on me over the years.

These days teams have a game plan and more or less stick to it rigidly. That has a down side, as players are afraid of doing something off the cuff in case it backfires and they end up getting a rollicking.

For example when I first came to Saints I used to chip and dribble the ball, but if I had tried to kick it late on in my career I would have been blasted. Even though they try and say everyone is multi-skilled, you are programmed like a robot with what you are doing.

It can be frustrating because you might know something is on, say a chip over on the third tackle, but you dare not do it. In that respect, the unexpected element has gone. We still have all the weapons, but only use one or two of them. Defences are getting stronger each year and it seems the only way of breaking them down is to get repeat sets and wait for fatigue to take its toll or the off-load to pull the line out of shape.

Certain players, particularly the half backs, still have licence to do what they want and their stuff is great if it comes off. But they get stick if it doesn't work. Imagine that try I scored against Bradford in the last seconds. Well if Longy's kick across had been intercepted he would have probably been slated!

There is a lot of talk about multi-skilling nowadays but the British forwards in the 70s could always pass a ball. I class multi-skilling as being able to pass a ball both ways, kick and tackle. It is not the ability to play second row, stand-off and centre! If you have to put a full-back to scrum half it means to me your squad has no strength in depth.

When I signed for Saints I had a reputation as a tries and breaks man, but then I turned into a tackler because of my fitness. I could have got away with doing 15 tackles less a match, but because you are in the thick of it you don't mind going again straight after you have made a tackle. There is so much emphasis nowadays on doing doubles and trebles on the tackle front.

For me it is going to be a transitional period from being a disciplined individual – and I can already see it slipping because I have been used to being regimented. From training or playing every day of the week, I no longer have to do that. My head still keeps telling me to go for a run or go to the gym.

It is hard to find a happy medium, because I don't need to be at the same level of fitness I was at last year. That is one of the biggest things I will miss, because I always enjoyed training.

Perhaps I won't be as enthusiastic in 10 years time – but my heart is a muscle and I have a big heart because I am used to training. I have to treat it as such and slowly let it adjust because it does not need to work as hard. Since finishing playing though, I have already lost half a stone.

There are a lot of people I need to pay tribute to for helping me in my career. My parents have been very supportive of me, although they have never watched a game at Knowsley Road. All my family are very modest and love to see me do well, but they have always kept that support in house so to speak.

Up at Saints there are dozens of people behind the scenes who have played their part in helping the club be successful.

I am sorry if I miss anybody out, but I would like to mention a few of those people who have assisted me behind the scenes.

People like Monica, who has sadly passed away, and Alice who used to wash the kit. Then there is Christine in the shop and Steph in the restaurant. I have built up good friendships with 'Toffee' Jack Coatsworth, Gibbsy, kitman Stan Wall and his predecessor Joe Mulcrow over the years.

Physios Janette Smith and Clare Mannion have been really helpful in my time at the club.

Former secretary Geoff Sutcliffe as been helping around the club for years and we should not forget Marge who was the players' best friend when dishing out the wages. We were all sorry to see her go. Alan Rooney has also been helpful to me while at the club.

Chairman Eamonn McManus has been absolutely great for Saints. He was alongside me at the conference when I announced my retirement. What I like about him is his straightness, which is a sadly rare commodity in sport these days. You can talk to him on a one to one basis and he will give you a solution or a way round a problem. He is a good bloke, who has helped restructure the club.

Chief executive Sean McGuire has also made a big impact. He has had a tough job to do, particularly with getting rid of players. He is not afraid of making tough decisions in the club's interest. Away from work he is a cracking bloke. Both Sean and Eamonn are Saints through and through and I think that is where they get their drive to succeed from.

Playing for Saints has opened doors for me to do other things over the years. Away from playing I have been involved in a couple of charity groups. An organisation called CALM, the *Campaign Against Living Miserably*, sent a newsletter to the club in 1999. The Merseyside and North West area has the highest suicide rate among young men. CALM is a 24-hour telephone helpline, where you can talk about debt, work or relationship problems.

My role was as an ambassador to raise awareness in the town – and Saints have been actively involved. You would see beer mats with the details on in some pubs – it was a case of getting the message across.

I have been involved with the *Prince's Trust* since about 1998. It is a fantastic organisation that helps many people across the country. St Helens has one of the most successful franchises – and it is not all about abseiling! If you pick up a paper it is always negative about youngsters, but these kids do a good job.

Everybody assumes I will naturally become a coach because I already have a coaching badge, but there are more jobs in rugby league than just coaching. I enjoy the mechanics of how the club and game is run because I have had to deal with matters like that as a captain.

There are a lot of other things around in the game, such as helping guide young ones down the correct career routes and there are other mentoring jobs there too.

The best players don't automatically make the best coaches, I have my own ideas on how the game should be played but I want to make sure any decision I make about the future is right for me and my family.

19

MY DREAM TEAM

I have had the privilege of playing alongside many great players during my career at Oldham, Saints and Newcastle Knights. After a lot of head scratching this is what I would offer up as my 'Dream Team' of the lads I have played alongside.

Full-back:
I played with some other top notch full-backs including long-serving Aussie Phil Veivers, who was a legend at Knowsley Road and Dave Lyon, who was one of the safest people under a bomb. If Wello had been around for a few years longer, he may have been in with a shout as well.

But I have to go for Gary Connolly as my full-back. Gary has been so consistent throughout his career. He is a tremendous player who I could have easily picked at centre also. As the years have rolled by, he has shown he can still produce the goods. He won the Lance Todd Trophy in 2003, which is not bad for a lad who first played at Wembley back in 1989! He is a special player.

Wing:
For my wingers, Anthony Sullivan has to be the first on the list. When Sully was on song if you gave him half a gap he was through and it would be 'Goodnight Vienna' – try time all the way. As part of our left-hand side gang, he would have to be number five.

The other spot would be between Les Quirk, Darren Albert, Alan Hunte and Mike Riley. Huntey on his day was lethal and when I started off at Saints he was on top form. He could be the cockiest bloke you could ever meet, but he was a flier, could also step off both feet and find the try line.

Centres:

For my first centre I would plump for my old buddy Paul Newlove, because he knew his way to the line and he was another part of our quartet down the left-hand channel, which was our bread and butter. On his day he was the best centre in world rugby, even if he was so laid back.

We have had plenty of really top class centres at Knowsley Road – Paul Loughlin, Scott Gibbs and Kevin Iro. But I have to go for Lockers, who was at Saints when I arrived and was a Great Britain international. He could kick goals from anywhere, which was unusual for a centre. He was also strong and quick, but what swings it for me was his unswerving loyalty to Saints. Without being disrespectful to the club, I know he could have gone to Wigan on numerous occasions. He is a great bloke.

Gibbsy was new to our game when he arrived, but he chucked himself into it and was one of the quickest learners. I only caught Kevin Iro towards the end of his career but he was a big game player. He knew which games he was ready for and there is no doubt he picked them.

Stand-off:

Tommy Martyn would be my automatic selection at stand-off. How he did not get an international cap is beyond me. Some said he was a poor defender, but in the latter part of his career he was one of the best tacklers in the game, and that is saying nothing of his Cumberland Throw. He was the other member of our left-sided gang. He was a fantastic player – not a robot, with Tommy everything was off the cuff.

Kiwi Tea Ropati was outstanding, particularly in the first year I was at Saints when he won First Division player of the year. Jonathan Griffiths was one of the fittest blokes I ever played with and would have been a world beater had he learned how to pass occasionally.

Scrum half:

Scrum half is a choice between Joey Johns, who I played with at Newcastle, Bobbie Goulding and Sean Long. Goulding, in his pomp, was a great player, motivator and he could win a game.

Johns was a phenomenal talent – everybody knows how good he is.

But I think I have to pick Longy because of his overall toughness. There are times over the past couple of years when I have seen Longy more or less roll his sleeves up and become a prop forward. That is what I like about him – it is not just his speed and astute kicking game, he is a tough dude as well. After the career threatening injuries he has had, it is amazing the way he has come back to be as good if not better than before.

Prop:

In the front row I have to put David Fairleigh's name down first even though he was only here for one season. He had a tremendous attitude and was very athletic for a forward. There was not that much on him, but he had a lot of attributes.

Even though I only played a year with Kevin Ward also, I would pick him as my other prop. They say front rowers had no brains, but he did and that is why he played the game at the top level for so long. He was a kind of minder for us during that first year, but he was a good bloke as well.

There were plenty of other good props to pick from too. Julian O'Neill should never have been released so early because he was so consistent and could take the knocks as well. Darren Britt was another one worthy of mention, a very strong runner who could slip the ball out. Big Cumbrian Jonathan Neill was also another bloke who was hard as nails.

Hooker:

Number nine is a choice between two St Helens lads – both fine servants to the town and rugby league – Bernard Dwyer or Keiron Cunningham. I have to pick Keiron because I have seen him develop into a phenomenal player during the Super League era. It is just a pity he has not appeared on the world stage a bit more.

Second row:

With me in the second row I would pick Sonny Nickle, who I have played alongside for both Saints and Great Britain. In the early 90s we both got plenty of plaudits, with him used as the battering ram and me as the runner. We complemented each other. There have been plenty of others – Darren Smith and Peter Shiels. George Mann was quite an unorthodox character, he was tough but once he got into his stride he could run as well. Local lad John Harrison was an unusual shape being 6ft 7ins, but was as tough as they come.

Loose forward:
At 13 – and I am probably biased – I have to pick Paul Sculthorpe ahead of Shane Cooper. Scully's ability to play anywhere swings it his way, although I know Coops was also quite versatile.

Even when Scully plays stand-off he acts like another loose forward and vice-versa. He has put in some fantastic performances over the years, and the victory over Brisbane in the World Club Challenge springs to mind.

Shane Cooper was Mr Magic, who played on till he was 105. I don't think even his wife knew his real age. He could really direct a team around a field like a traffic policeman.

Dream team:
1. Gary Connolly
2. Alan Hunte
3. Paul Loughlin
4. Paul Newlove
5. Anthony Sullivan
6. (20) Tommy Martyn
7. Sean Long
8. Kevin Ward
9. Keiron Cunningham
10. David Fairleigh
11. Chris Joynt
12. Sonny Nickle
13. Paul Sculthorpe

In terms of opposition players who have shone against me particularly I would probably select either Kris Radlinski or Darren Lockyer at full back. Lockyer is always in the right place at the right time – and has helped snatch series wins from GB over the past five years.

Wings would be Jason Robinson, a very elusive player, and flier Martin Offiah on the other.

Centres would be the two Aussie giants Gene Miles and Mal Meninga. With Meninga it was a case of getting in his road.

The *half back* combination would be Shaun Edwards at stand-off – a tough player with skill, pace and vision – and Joey Johns at scrum half.

My first *prop* would be 'The Chief' Paul Harrogan, and the other one would be Terry O'Connor, as long as he does not wear white boots. Terry is a very under-rated player. When we toured New Zealand we were sponsored by Puma and they were giving free boots away. Well he came back with these white boots. He said, 'Should I wear them in the test match?' He looked a real poser in them – and he ended up getting bounced! I should also thank him for the ironing he used to do on tour.

Lee Jackson would be the *hooker* because he was lightning in his pomp, and really effective around the ruck, even though there was more meat on Good Friday than on him!

I would have to find a place for Jason Smith in there somewhere because he was outstanding.

In the *second row* would be Andrew Farrell, a player I have enjoyed many tussles with over the years, and Brisbane and Aussie Gordon Tallis

Brad Fittler would be the *loose forward*.

POSTSCRIPT

This is probably a strange way to end an autobiography but I would like to outline the way I want to leave this earth!

Being a Catholic I have seen the church change over the years and been to many different funerals. I would not want my funeral to be a morbid affair; instead I would want it to be a celebration of my life.

I would make sure there was a few bob set aside in my will to make sure that it happened in one of my local pubs. I think an Irish band would have to be hired for the occasion so the 'mourners' could sing to their hearts' content.

There would be no full requiem mass because they tend to go on too long – just a nice, short sharp service with a couple of my best buddies giving a speech.

I just want everybody to remember me as a good 'un in his day, good father and family man and who enjoyed life and a few pints along the way.

I intend to be buried, not cremated, and am sure somebody will pick a few hymns, but would like them to play a song like 'Fields of Athenry', not because I am political, but because it is a good tune. They can carry me out to 'Pebbles on a Beach' by my favourite artist Paul Weller or maybe 'Going Underground' by The Jam might be more appropriate as they cart me up to the cemetery.

I don't know what I'd have carved on my tombstone – but one thing is for sure, 2002 Grand Final referee Russell Smith won't be standing over the grave saying, 'Get up and play on, Joynty!'

TRIBUTES

Paul Wellens (Saints)

One of Chris's great qualities is having time for people, and especially young players. Chris was brilliant with me when I first made it into the first team and other young players like Mike Bennett, Mark Edmondson and Tim Jonkers will all say the same. He went to great lengths to tell me that if I needed any help or advice he would help me out.

Tommy Martyn (Oldham, Saints and Ireland)

Chris is a natural leader, with great knowledge, who commands real respect.

Away from the rugby field Chris does lots of charity work, but always shies away from any publicity that could go with it. Some people do charity work for pats on the back, but any showboating Chris does is in his head. Like with his rugby, he just gets the job done.

Mal Reilly (former Great Britain and Newcastle Knights coach)

Chris is a natural player, who is very honest with it. I believe his valuable and positive contribution on the park has on many occasion been the difference between Saints winning and losing – and unfortunately my teams have been on the receiving end of that so many times.

When I was coaching Newcastle Knights during 1995, Chris did a very solid job for us. I was very disappointed when St Helens recalled him before the end of the season, because he could have made a difference in the play-offs.

Shaun McRae (Former Saints coach)

From a playing point of view Chris is among the upper echelons of the players I have worked with in the game. A mark of a good player is not letting the captain's job affect your own game – it is not easy to do what Chris has done, yet he remained as consistent as ever.

Paul Newlove (Saints and Great Britain)

Me and Chris formed quite a bit of a deadly partnership up that left flank and it has been rewarding for us both, and the team, over the years. On the field Chris has everything you want – ability, good hands, great sidestep and tremendous work rate.

Tony Barrow (former coach at Oldham)

As a player you think of his great positional sense. In some ways he is like Ellery Hanley, knowing where the ball is going to pop up. How many times has he been there in the big games like Brisbane and Bradford to grab that crucial score?

You can add to that some tremendous defensive stints and what a job he has done as captain. He gives real credence to the saying actions speak louder than words.

Bernard Dwyer (Saints, Bradford and Great Britain)

Joynty always caught the eye with his wide running and attacking flair, but what impressed me most was his defensive stints. Joynty earned my respect as a team-mate and certainly as an opponent in my time as a Bulls player. I always looked forward to coming up against him on the field and know the feeling was mutual.

Kris Radlinski (Wigan and GB)

I played alongside Chris with Great Britain on a number of occasions and when Chris speaks, everyone listens. Not many people have that power.

You can always count on Joynty to pull out the big play when his team needs it. Joynty is a tough player, a great leader, but a better bloke – oh yes and a Wiganer!

Scott Gibbs (former Saints centre)

I have played with and against many great players and Chris ranks up there with some of the best, especially in the way he applies himself.

Playing and training alongside him, and some of the other guys at St Helens, was a real pleasure from a professional and personal standpoint.

Brian Noble (Bradford Bulls and Great Britain coach)

Chris is one of those people who have continually embarrassed Bradford sides at the right stage of the game. On the field he is a class act, one of the people that we coaches like to rely on. His performances are as reliable as a quartz clock. He is an outstanding leader and a true champion and as an individual he is instrumental in creating the right environment for the 'Team' ethic. Chris Joynt is what I would describe as one of those 'Silverbacks' that Coaches rely on.

Ian Millward (Saints coach)

Chris wants to continually challenge himself even though he has earned the highest accolades in the game. He won't accept second best off himself or other players. That had a huge impact on our other high profile players as well as our youngsters. He is very hard-nosed in regard to achieving those goals and a very calm person who is not flustered by adversity.

Paul Sculthorpe (Saints and Great Britain)

We have had a great deal of success at Saints, but there is a real level-headedness in the camp. A lot of that is down to Chris. He has achieved everything in the game and yet he has always kept his feet firmly on the ground.

David Waite (former Great Britain coach)

Chris has undoubted playing ability, but that is complemented by a mental toughness, great preparation and attention to the needs of the team.

He is calm, composed and a natural leader. He is the ultimate team player and that is why he commands so much respect.

When Chris finishes playing, I feel it is important that he is not lost to game of rugby league. He has so much to give – and would make an outstanding contribution as a coach if that is what he wanted to do.

Dave Lyon (former Saints full back and England Academy coach)
Chris has emerged to become a modern great within the history of St Helens, but he is also level-headed, humble and never forgotten his roots, making him popular with not only the players and staff, but also the fans.

He is genuine, sincere and it has been a privilege to share some of the club's triumphs in his company.

APPENDIX

Chris Joynt career statistics

Honours

25 caps for Great Britain (2 tries)

1996 Lions Tour (2 additional mid week games)

1999 Lions Tour (1 additional mid week game)

6 caps for England (2 tries), 1992–96

4 caps for Ireland (1 try), 2000 World Cup

2 caps for Lancashire

4 caps for Great Britain Under 21s (1 try), 1991–93

Coaches Select XIII – 1994–95

Super League Dream Team – 1999

Young Player of the Year Runner-Up – 1992–93

1993 and 2000 Harry Sunderland Award Winner

Man of the Match in the 2001 World Club Challenge

World Club Challenge Winner: 2001

Super League Grand Final Winner: 1999, 2000 & 2002

Super League Championship Winner: 1996

Challenge Cup Winner: 1996, 1997, 2001 & 2004

Premiership Trophy Winner: 1992-93

World Club Challenge Runner Up: 2000 & 2003

1st Division Championship Runner Up: 1992–93

Challenge Cup Runner Up: 2002

Premiership Trophy Runner Up: 1997

Regal Trophy Runner Up: 1995–96

Lancashire Cup Final Runner Up: 1992–93

Stones Divisional Premiership Trophy Runner Up: 1991–92

Career Record

Signed for Oldham from Wigan St Patricks ARL on 27 April 1989.

Debut: Oldham v Carlisle (Sub), Watersheddings on 8 April 1990. Won 48–16.

First Oldham try: v St Helens, Lancashire Cup 2nd Round, Knowsley Road on 26 September 1991. Lost 26–39.

Joined St Helens on 2 September 1992.

Debut: St Helens v Wakefield Trinity (Sub), Knowsley Road on 6 September 1992. Won 24–12.

First St Helens try: v Huddersfield, Regal Trophy Preliminary Round, Knowsley Road on 27 October 1992. Won 44–18.

Great Britain debut: v France (Sub), Carcassonne on 7 March 1993. Won 48–6.

First Great Britain try: v France, Agen on 26 October 2001 Won 42–12

	App		T	G	DG	Pts
Playing Record						
Oldham	28	(24+4)	10	-	-	40
St. Helens	382	(363+19)	121	-	-	484
Newcastle	7	(4+3)	1	-	-	4
Great Britain	25	(19+6)	2	-	-	8
'96 Tour	2	-	-	-	-	-
'99 Tour	1	-	-	-	-	-
England	6	(3+3)	2	-	-	8
Ireland	4	-	1	-	-	4
Lancashire	2	-	-	-	-	-
GB U-21s	4	(3+1)	1	-	-	4
Totals	**461**	**(425+36)**	**138**	**-**	**-**	**552**

First Team players Chris Joynt has appeared with

St Helens

Adam Fogerty, Ade Gardner, Alan Cross, Alan Hunte, Andy Bracek, Andy Dannatt, Andy Haigh, Andy Leathem, Andy Northey, Anthony Fenlon, Anthony Sullivan, Apollo Perelini, Augustine O'Donnell, Barry Ward, Bernard Dwyer, Bobbie Goulding, Brett Goldspink, Brian Capewell, Brian Henare, Carl Forber, Chris Giles, Chris Morley, Chris Newall, Chris Smith, Damien Smith, Danny Arnold, Darrell Trindall, Darren Albert, Darren Britt, Darren Smith, Dave McConnell, Dave Whittle, David Fairleigh, David Lyon, Dean Busby, Derek McVey, Des Clark, Dom Feaunati, Dwayne West, Fereti Tuilagi, Gareth Cunningham, Gareth Price, Gary Connolly, George Mann, Gray Viane, Heath Cruckshank, Ian Connor, Ian Hardman, Ian Kenny, Ian Pickavance, James Arkwright, James Graham, James Roby, Jarrod McCracken, Jason Hooper, Jason Johnson, Jason Roach, Joey Hayes, John Braddish, John Hamilton, John Harrison, John Hill, John Kirkpatrick, John McAttee, John Stankevitch, Jon Simms,

Jon Wilkin, Jonathan Griffiths, Jonathan Neill, Julian O'Neill, Karle Hammond, Keiron Cunningham, Keith Mason, Kevin Iro, Kevin O'Loughlin, Kevin Ward, Lee Briers, Lee Gilmour, Leon Felton, Les Quirk, Liam Bostock, Mark Edmondson, Mark Elia, Mark McCully, Martin Gleeson, Martin Walker, Maurie Fa'asavalu, Micky Higham, Mike Bennett, Mike Riley, Mike Roby, Nick Devine, Nick Fozzard, Paul Anderson, Paul Atcheson, Paul Davidson, Paul Forber, Paul Groves, Paul Loughlin, Paul Mathison, Paul Newlove, Paul Sculthorpe, Paul Southern, Paul Wellens, Peaufai Leuila, Peter Atherton, Peter Cook, Peter Shiels, Phil Adamson, Phil Anderton, Phil Veivers, Phil Waring, Radney Bowker, Richard Sheil, Ricky Bibey, Ricky Cowan, Scott Barrow, Scott Gibbs, Scott Moore, Sean Casey, Sean Hoppe, Sean Long, Shane Cooper, Simon Booth, Sonny Nickle, Stephen Prescott, Steve Hall, Steve Maden, Steve Rowlands, Stuart Jones, Tea Ropati, Tim Jonkers, Tommy Hodgkinson, Tommy Martyn, Tony Stewart, Vila Matautia, Wayne McDonald, Willie Talau.

Oldham

Shaun Allen, Tony Anderson, Keith Atkinson, Mick Bardsley, Ian Bates, Leo Casey, Brett Clarke, Neil Clawson, John Cogger, Trevor Croston, John Fairbank, John Fieldhouse, Neil Flanagan, Mike Ford, Des Foy, John Henderson, Gary Hyde, Richard Irving, Peter Lewis, Paul Lord, Tommy Martyn, John Maxwell, Charlie McAlister, Kevin Meadows, Keith Newton, Duncan Platt, Steve Robinson, Paul Round, Andy Ruane, Richard Russell, Ian Sanderson, Tony Barrow, Richard Blackman, Austin Donegan, Ronnie Duane, Norman Francis, Simon Longstaff, Derek Pyke, Steve Warburton, Jeff Bimson, David Bradbury, Paul Buckley, Ged Byrne, Gary Christie, Mike Clements, Tony Conroy, Logan Edwards, Joe Faimalo, Joe Grima, Neil Holding, Brett Jones, Barrie McDermott, Mark Mulligan, Vince Nicklin, Richard Pachniuk, Scott Ranson, Iva Ropati, Ian Sherratt, David Stephenson, Tim Street, Shane Tupaea, Sean Tyrer.